爺 垃 圾 孤
注 意 宝 貝 狂 者 的 什 么 胡 扯 真 他 媽
統 手 故 障 檢 查 氧 氣 供 應 你 好 天 曉 得 凶 殘
殺 手 廢 物 平 靜 哎 呀 坏 了 閉 嘴
很 不 體 貼 的 男 生 不 體 貼 的 男 生 救 生
殘 殺 手 是 你 的 慢 慢 的 闌 彈 醬 完 美 猫 目
若 木 雞 藍 日 你 告 訴 那 牛 它 有 双 美
地 獄 的 嬡 子 的 媽 茶 快 去 很 遠 的 地 方
發 婦 神 圣 的 睪 丸 她 是 所
交 的 藏

firefly

The Gorramn Shiniest

DICTIONARY and PHRASEBOOK

in the 'Verse

FIREFLY:
The Gorramn Shiniest Dictionary
and Phrasebook in the 'Verse

ISBN 9781783298617

Published by Titan Books
A division of Titan Publishing Group Ltd
144 Southwark Street
London
SE1 0UP

United Kingdom

First edition: March 2016

Printed in China

2 4 6 8 10 9 7 5 3 1

Did you enjoy this book? We love to hear from our readers.
Please e-mail us at: **readerfeedback@titanemail.com**
or write to **Reader Feedback** at the above address.

To receive advance information, news, competitions, and exclusive
offers online, please sign up for the Titan newsletter on our website:
www.titanbooks.com

A CIP catalogue record for this title is available from the British Library.

CONTENTS

TITANBOOKS

Abbreviations Used

As you peruse this guide to the words and phrases used in the *Firefly* TV show, you'll notice that there are abbreviations next to each entry. These abbreviations refer to the following:

abbr.	abbreviation	*pl.*	plural
adj.	adjective	*pr.adj.*	proper adjective
adv.	adverb	*pr.*	pronoun
fem.	feminine	*pr.n.*	proper noun
id.	idiomatic phrase	*sing.*	singular
interj.	interjection	*sl.*	slang
lc.	lowercase	*up.*	uppercase
masc.	masculine	*v.*	verb
n.	noun	*vul.*	vulgar

Language Use in the 'Verse

In the *Firefly* TV show, the characters' use of language is as unique and diverse as the cultures that span hundreds of planets and moons throughout the 'Verse. Though Earth-That-Was boasted thousands of different languages and dialects, including English and Mandarin Chinese, the 'Verse's burgeoning population is an even bigger cultural mish-mash filled with literate and illiterate folk who have adopted and internalized their own way of speaking. The words people speak reflect more than their ability to hold a conversation or convey information; they also indicate where people are from, what their culture is, and, in some cases, what their beliefs and personalities are like, too. That, when combined with the fact that the show takes place over 500 years into the future, implies that the use of language has evolved and shifted to reflect futuristic worlds. Thus, Captain Malcolm Reynolds and the eight *Serenity* crewmembers are written with their own unique voices that paint a picture of what life is like in 2517.

The English words and phrases presented in this guide narrow in on these concepts and characters to reflect the experiences of a twenty-sixth-century citizen in the world of *Firefly*. When combined, the individual entries form a picture of the 'Verse that presents how Joss Whedon and his team of writers approached the stylistic use of language to ground viewers in the setting. Many of the technology-based words that refer to high-tech medicine, ship parts, and futuristic science were created specifically for the show. Others, like the military, political, and religious terms, are a blend of real-world definitions that were spun in a fresh direction

to show how society has evolved in these areas. Lastly, the English curse words, insults, and colloquialisms are drawn from nineteenth-century Americana and Victorian England to give the show a feeling of being on the frontier (or Border planets).

One way to frame language usage is to focus on how characters speak depending on where they're from: Core, Border or rim. Each section of the 'Verse has positive and negative stereotype related to how people speak. For example, living in the heart of the 'Verse has a profound psychological impact on characters due to the White Sun System's or Central planets' wealth, government, and physical location. The Anglo-Sino Alliance, which is based in the Core, is omnipresent and its influence can be felt on every planet and moon. Combined, characters from the Core, like Simon Tam and Inara Serra, are well-educated and speak formally using correct grammar and proper titles, like "Captain". This style of language use is influenced by status, economic background, and internalized social mores and pressures. Vocabulary that includes slang, colloquialisms, and cursing is not typically used by either character. Cursing, especially, is rarely part of a Core character's everyday speech and is considered taboo. Inara, for example, upbraids Atherton Wing in "Shindig" for his improper use of language at the dance.

Both the Border planets and the rim are interesting in the sense that the exact opposite is true of them. While folk from the Core "speak properly", people who live in the Border and rim use contractions, alternate spellings of words, abbreviations, odd turns of phrase, and a variety of colorful curse words in everyday communication. Cursing is not frowned upon and, in some cases, people who don't curse are considered stuck up or overly formal. Border and rim natives negatively stereotype the grammatically correct speakers, while the opposite is also true. People from the Core believe that settlers in the Border and rim planets are backwards and unintelligent because they don't speak in a classic manner befitting someone of a higher social standing or an educated background. This dichotomy of language creates friction between the two types of speakers, as can be seen amongst *Serenity's* crew. For specific language tips related to each of the *Serenity* crewmembers, turn to their personal pages (see contents) for guidance.

In addition to the use of English, the *Firefly* writers also employed Chinese in their scripts. We explore this on pages 136-9 of the book with *Firefly* TV translator Jenny Lynn. Her Q & A covers the use of the Chinese language in the show and is followed by the English-to-Chinese translations for each episode, including never-before-seen bonus translations. Shiny!

A.M.I., *pr.n. abbr.* Prestigious medical facility found on Osiris in the White Sun System.

A.T.V., *n. abbr.* All-terrain vehicle. Small A.T.V.s are favored by spacefarers due to their compact size. They can be easily stored and secured in a ship's cargo hold.

abbess, *n. fem.* Female head of an abbey and its congregation.

abbey, *n.* On Earth-That-Was, an abbey referred to a Christian monastery or nunnery filled with devotees that pray, study, and typically contribute to a local community by providing religious services or other acts of charity. In the 'Verse, abbeys continue to be a pillar of the community and are filled with Christian preachers called "Shepherds" who live and pray in a complex. Buildings may include a small church, gardens, a library, living quarters, etc. While abbeys can be built anywhere, they tend to be found in or near civilized areas within the White Sun System and are an integral part of society.

abbot, *n. masc.* Male head of an abbey and its congregation.

Academy, *pr.n.* 1. Place of learning. Academies can be found on the Central Planets or wherever the Alliance has a strong foothold. *pr.n.* 2. On the surface, promoted as a government-run school for gifted students who live in the Central Planets. Students are trained to become unwitting government assassins and spies, and may be subjected to human experimentation in order to trigger enhanced mental or biological traits. They are prevented from making direct contact with their families and friends. River Tam is a former Academy student. *n. lc.* 3. Non-specific school or college.

There was a school … a, uh, government-sponsored Academy, we'd never even heard of it but it had the most exciting program, the most challenging… We could have sent her anywhere, we had the money … but she wanted to go. She wanted to learn. She was fourteen."

– Simon Tam, "Serenity"

adrenaline, *n.* Synthetic or natural drug used to stimulate the heart in emergency situations. Often injected straight into the heart with a hypodermic needle. Mal shot himself full of adrenaline in "Out of Gas".

aeronautics, *n.* 1. Broad field of study

that includes all technical and physical aspects of flight and that takes place in and above a planetary or lunar atmosphere. Pilots and captains are expected to be proficient in this area. *n.* 2. Ship system concerned with navigation and spaceflight. Interference and problems may occur if the ship's technology is old or outdated when compared with the newer tech found in the Core.

aft, *adj.* Toward, or at, the tail end of a spaceship, e.g. "The aftdeck hall is just past the crew's quarters."

aged, *adj.* Natural maturation that takes place over time. Usually refers to alcohol or specific foods, like cheese. Liqueurs, wines, and spirits that are naturally aged are expensive to produce and to buy.

air support, *n.* Military assistance, typically in the form of bombs and cover fire, provided to troops stationed on the ground.

airlock, *n.* Tunnel or chamber that allows crewmembers to travel between one ship and another in space, without suffering from a change in air pressure or airflow. Typically, the airlock is operated in a specific sequence of events by opening one door at a time to prevent air from escaping from the pressurized vessel. A temporary airlock may also be constructed to connect one spaceship to another, to permit safe travel between ships.

Airxoen, Miles, M.D., *pr.n.* Alias Malcolm Reynolds used to enter St Lucy's Medical Center in Ariel City during the hospital heist in "Ariel".

alcohol, *n.* Common mood-altering substance created by the fermentation of starches or sugars. May be produced naturally or synthetically, and combined with other substances. Bars, taverns, and saloons that serve alcohol can be found on every habitable planet or moon throughout the 'Verse.

alert, *n.* Warning broadcast widely, usually across public communication channels.

aliens, *n. pl.* Extraterrestrial beings from outer space that were once thought to live among the stars. Though their existence has been soundly disproven, some still have the misguided belief they are real.

Alliance, *pr.adj.* 1. Term used to describe government owned, sanctioned, or run objects, facilities, services, or people, e.g. "Them's Alliance goods." *pr.n. abbr.* 2. Short form of Anglo-Sino Alliance. Commonly used.

Alliance cruiser, *pr.n.* Massive, high tech military vessel the size of a small city that is owned and operated by the Alliance. The Tohoku-class is noted for its size, population, and unusual shape. Five interconnected towers protrude from the u-shaped bottom of the cruiser to form this "floating city". It was designed to function as a cross between a space station, like Li Shen's Space Bazaar, and a military headquarters. In addition to their scientific, military, medical, engineering, recreational, and storage facilities, Alliance cruisers have the capacity to hold dozens of Alliance gunships and are fully equipped to survive extended trips in space. Typically, Alliance cruisers can be found patrolling the Border planets and the rim. While they can and do perform rescue missions, their primary purpose is to keep the peace in a sector by searching for fugitives, illegal salvagers, and other criminally-minded individuals that have either run afoul of the law or threaten the stability of the Alliance. Though the cruiser moves more slowly than its gunships, the ship is outfitted with a tractor beam to forcibly draw a targeted vessel towards its hull. When the boat is in range, a temporary airlock is extended to the captured boat, allowing the Alliance to safely board it.

"Alliance said they were gonna waltz through Serenity Valley and we've choked 'em with those words. We've done the impossible and that makes us mighty. Just a little while longer, our angels'll be soaring overhead, raining fire on those arrogant cods, so you hold! You HOLD!" – Malcolm Reynolds, "Serenity"

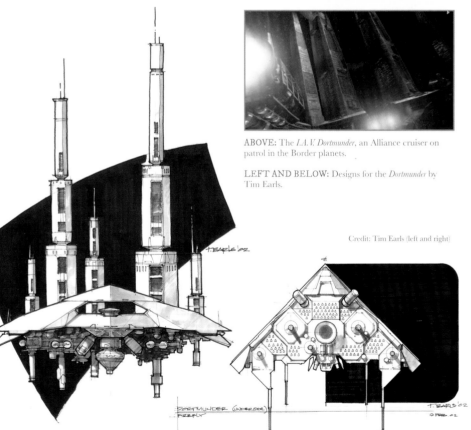

ABOVE: The *I.A.V. Dortmunder*, an Alliance cruiser on patrol in the Border planets.

LEFT AND BELOW: Designs for the *Dortmunder* by Tim Earls.

Credit: Tim Earls (left and right)

Credit: Charles Ratteray

Alliance gunship, *pr.n.* 1. Small, heavily armed, short-range vessel engineered to support an Alliance cruiser. The gunship is slightly larger than the average shuttle, but has more munitions and seats fewer personnel. One ship is more maneuverable and faster than a cruiser, but isn't powerful enough to take on a larger ship without assistance. Typically, Alliance gunships are flown in configurations of two or more depending upon the circumstance. *pr.n.* 2. Refers to a general type of ship designed by the Alliance military to be used in times of war or conflict, regardless of the vessel's size or class. In the Unification War, Alliance gunships were flown in every battle.

Alliance police shuttle, *pr.n.* Small, short-range vessel used by Alliance law enforcement stationed in or near a municipality found on a planet or moon. The police shuttle was designed to patrol the surface, is about the size of a hovercar, and can only transport up to four people. On Bellerophon, police shuttles are clearly marked and equipped with alarms. They are akin to a private security force on that planet, and will respond to emergency signals triggered by the elite from their island estates.

Alliance Short Range Enforcement Vessel or **A.S.R.E.V.,** *pr.n. abbr.* Type of spaceship operated by official government representatives, usually federal marshalls, to track criminals and patrol specific regions of space. The ship is small, maneuverable,

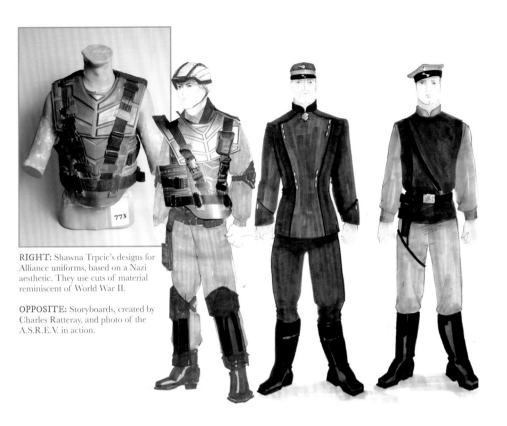

RIGHT: Shawna Trpcic's designs for Alliance uniforms, based on a Nazi aesthetic. They use cuts of material reminiscent of World War II.

OPPOSITE: Storyboards, created by Charles Ratteray, and photo of the A.S.R.E.V. in action.

heavily-armed, and can travel at high speeds. Munitions include missiles, hull-piercing bullets, and magnetic depth charges. Flown in "The Message" by Lieutenant Womack to Li Shen's Space Bazaar, and later to the freezing cold planet of St Albans in the Red Sun System.

Alliance uniform, *pr.n.* Distinctive garments worn by Alliance military forces signifying rank and position. Most Alliance military organizations have at least two standardized uniforms: one for everyday use and another for formal occasions. Colors are utilitarian: steel gray, white, tan, light gray, and black.

Allied, *pr.adj.* Used interchangeably with Alliance when describing objects, systems, facilities, or services.

Allied Enforcement, *pr.n.* Official title for a government-run law enforcement agency. Womack, who appears in "The Message", holds the rank of Lieutenant.

Allied postal system, *pr.n.* A twenty-sixth-century equivalent of a federal post office. Ammon Duul is the postmaster at Li Shen's Space Bazaar. Shipping corpses, according to Lieutenant Womack, is illegal.

Alliance propaganda, *pr.n.* Biased information relaying a carefully crafted image of the Alliance and its actions to further the goals and desires of its political leaders. Propaganda may be overt, subtle, or subliminal, and is typically designed to relay how wonderful and beneficial the government is to humanity. The frequency and density of distributed messages depends upon the system. Alliance propaganda is stronger in the Core than on the rim. While the propaganda is successful, the government's illicit and inhumane actions are not unknown to its citizens, even in the Central planets. Gabriel Tam alludes to this during Simon's flashback in "Safe".

alprazaline push, *n.* Drug administered to constrict blood vessels.

"Amazing Grace", *pr.n.* Late eighteenth-century Christian hymn from Earth-That-Was. "Amazing Grace" is sung by Lucy at Nandi's funeral in "Heart of Gold". The song was written by John Newton in 1779.

ambassador, *n.* 1. Well-respected representative of a moon or planet who speaks on behalf of, or negotiates for, others. *n. sl.* 2. Sarcastic title. Companions are well respected in the Core and tend to have strong ties to the Alliance. Because they are viewed as loyalists, a Companion's presence benefits criminals, illegal salvagers, smugglers, and former Independents whose views and actions are questionable to law enforcement and members of the social elite. Though a Companion is helpful to have on board, the title is meant as a slight. Mal calls Inara an ambassador in "Serenity".

Amazing Grace
・--------∞--------・

Amazing grace! How sweet the sound,
That sav'd a wretch like me!
I once was lost, but now am found,
Was blind, but now I see.
'Twas grace that taught my heart to fear,
And grace my fears reliev'd;
How precious did that grace appear
The hour I first believ'd!

Thro' many dangers, toils, and snares,
I have already come;
'Tis grace hath brought me safe thus far,
And grace will lead me home.

The Lord has promis'd good to me,
His word my hope secures;
He will my shield and portion be
As long as life endures.

Yes, when this flesh and heart shall fail,
And mortal life shall cease;
I shall possess, within the veil,
A life of joy and peace.

The earth shall soon dissolve like snow,
The sun forbear to shine;
But God, who call'd me here below,
Will be forever mine.

ABOVE: The "Ariel" ambulance built from discarded parts. Its design originated from a mock-up of a helicopter fuselage.

ambulance, *n.* Vehicle used to fly patients to hospitals operating in the Central planets. In "Ariel", the hospital transport Wash and Kaylee fabricated was painted in white and bore a red insignia.

amygdala, *n.* Almond-shaped area of the brain responsible for regulating fear and aggression. Simon discovered River's amygdala had been operated on in an experimental procedure during "Ariel".

angels, *n. pl. sl.* Piloted ships that assist soldiers on the ground by bombing or firing upon enemy targets from above.

"That's our angels, come to blow the Alliance right to the hot place."

– Malcolm Reynolds, "Serenity"

— ⋅ —————— ⟨⟩⟨⟩⟨⟩ —————— ⋅ —

Anglo-Sino Alliance, *pr.n.* Governing body that oversees the Union of Allied Planets. Its reach encompasses all celestial bodies in this sector of space, which spans five systems. The Alliance is a neo-fascist government run by a parliament that is a blend of the twentieth-century American and Chinese political systems from Earth-That-Was. Its leaders are primarily located in the Central planets on Sihnon and Londinium, the 'Verse's capital planets. While the top-positioned rulers tend to remain within the Core, major and minor dignitaries can be found on the Border planets and rim, like Magistrate Higgins who runs Higgins' Moon and the

Councilor who coordinates with Ezra's World Councilor. Most people have strong feelings about the Alliance, one way or the other, due to their role in the Unification War that ended in 2511. The Unification War, which was instigated by the Alliance, was fought over the philosophy that the planetary systems would be better off under one governing body than a series of separate political systems. People within the Core often believed that the wealth, resources, and opportunities they enjoyed would be brought to the Border planets and rim if Unification came to pass. However, in a post-war environment income inequality is greater than ever, since the worlds outside the Core suffered the greatest losses during the conflict and jobs are scarce. Because the Alliance has a strong foothold in the Core, its interest in the Border and rim waxes and wanes according to its shifting priorities. It has made many attempts to encourage Alliance loyalists to colonize the Border and rim, but has not been successful overall. Dignitaries, like a prefect or a magistrate, are given more power in the Border than they would have in the Core for this reason, as the

— ⋅ —————— ⟨⟩⟨⟩⟨⟩ —————— ⋅ —

"You know what they say: history is programmed by the winners."
– Simon Tam, *"Serenity"*

government is anxious to settle and expand its reach. The Alliance's power, however, is hindered by the fact that terraforming isn't always successful, which sickens a local population, like the miners on Regina that provide cheap labor. Combined, these factors lead to a ruling body that is viewed very differently by folk outside the Core. The Anglo-Sino Alliance has a strong military presence that is felt by way of the patrols of Alliance cruisers and different types of law officials, like federal marshalls and lieutenants, which are both used to punish transgressors. It uses a variety of propaganda techniques and errs on the side of caution and paranoia to protect its interests, using technology and biological warfare to experiment on its citizens before putting them to good use, as was the case with River Tam. Though it may seem infallible, the Alliance is plagued by corruption. Also, the Unification War has left many scars that have yet to be healed, and groups of underground resistance fighters are not fooled by government propaganda. Working to its advantage, however, is its considerable size and the fact that its resources are vast. Its intimidating presence, which is felt throughout the 'Verse, keeps the majority of its citizens in check.

anti-aircraft gun, *n.* Munitions engineered to cripple or crash an enemy ship. Typically mounted on a base that can swivel 360 degrees. May be attached to a permanent structure, like a ship, or transported in a vehicle to match the speeds of a target. Rance Burgess uses an anti-aircraft gun in "Heart of Gold". One also appeared in Jayne's flashback during "Jaynestown". *n.* 2. Type of weapon used in the Unification War. Used in "Serenity".

aphasia, *n.* Condition that affects the brain's language center and removes the ability to speak, write, and understand written and verbal language. Caused by stroke, head injury, and other forms of brain damage. May be temporary or permanent.

aphasic, *n.* 1. Sufferer of aphasia. *adj.* 2. Related to or describing a state of aphasia.

Ariel, *pr.n.* Planet in the White Sun System.

Ariel City, *pr.n.* Major metropolis and notable hub of activity in the Central planets. Ariel City is located on Ariel in the White Sun System. It boasts many attractions including a bioluminescent lake and Bathgate Abbey, as well as commercial skyscrapers and municipal buildings like St Lucy's Medical Center. As in most well-populated cities in the Core, the Alliance is omnipresent here and easily accessible. For this reason, common problems that exist outside the Central planets, like vagrancy or drug addiction and abuse, are not visible to the naked eye. Though the Alliance has a strong presence here, an underground movement may also be found with the proper connections. The episode "Ariel" took place in this city.

asteroid belt, *n.* Celestial chunks of rock orbiting the space between planets in a ring.

Astra 400, *pr.n.* Manufacturer and model of the government-issued gun Lawrence Dobson uses in "Serenity".

ate his own gun, *id. masc.* Committing suicide by placing the front of a gun barrel on the roof of the mouth and pulling the trigger. Sheriff Bourne describes how Joey Bloggs ate his own gun in "The Train Job".

Athens, *pr.n.* Planet in the Georgia System that orbits the sun Huang Long. Whitefall is one of its four moons.

atmo feed, *n.* Part related to maintaining a ship's atmosphere at proper oxygen levels. Required to sustain human life in space.

atropine, *n.* Drug manufactured from the belladonna plant. Typically administered to surgical patients in order to stabilize their heart rate.

aught, *n.* Numerical value of zero.

aught three, *n.* Firefly ship model.

BOOK: She don't look like much.

KAYLEE: She'll fool ya. Ever sail in a Firefly?

BOOK: Long before you were crawling. Not an aught three, though. Didn't have the extenders, tended to shake.

– "Serenity"

ABOVE: *Serenity* lands at the bustling Ariel City docks. The high-tech landscape is typical of a Core city.
OPPOSITE: The anti-aircraft gun Mal fires up in "Serenity", during the Unification War-ending Battle of Serenity.

authorization, *n.* Permission granted by a ruling entity to conduct a variety of simple and complex tasks, like landing in a spaceport or visiting a government building.

authorization code, *n.* Cipher that is designed to grant security or military personnel permission to order and execute a specific command. An example of an Independent Lieutenant's authorization code is 56-9BKR-0 S47 LT LT.090-39R.

automated, *adj.* Describes objects that are programmed via a control panel to function independently of an operator, like the automated trash bins from "Trash".

autopilot, *n.* Navigational system that allows a pilot or captain to program a flight path into the ship's console. The ship will then automatically fly to that destination at a steady pace. Autopilot is used to conserve fuel and give crewmembers a break from the controls.

autopsy, *n.* Study conducted on a corpse to investigate how that person died. Simon Tam attempted to perform an autopsy on Tracey Smith in "The Message".

auxiliary, *adj.* Secondary, back-up, or reserve. On a ship, refers to a system or a part, e.g. "Plug that end into the auxiliary port."

B.P., *n.abbr.* Medical abbreviation for blood pressure.

backbirth or **backwater birth,** *n. vul.* Negative stereotype of a person born in an isolated town or rural settlement far removed from civilization. Similar to redneck or hick. Many people who live in the Central planets have the impression that anyone outside of the Core is a backbirth. Used as an insult.

badge, *n.* Symbol of authority used by law enforcement. The shape and design of the badge varies based on rank and the enforcer's unit or agency.

Badger, *pr.n.* Middleman and aspiring crime boss who operates out of a dingy office in Eavesdown Docks on Persephone. Originally from the Dyton Colony, Badger speaks with a thick English accent and wears a suit, tie, and bowler hat to reflect the appearance of a businessman. While Badger is a shady opportunist, he is a steady source of employment for the crew and provides them with smuggling jobs. Appeared in "Serenity" and "Shindig".

BADGER: Captain Reynolds. Heard you was in town. Thought we might have a bit of a sit-down.
MAL: I'd prefer a bit of a "piss-off".
BADGER: I'm very sorry. Did I give you the impression I was asking?
– "Shindig"

Balinese, *pr.n.* 1. Ethnic group of people who

can trace their roots back to the Indonesian
island of Bali on Earth-That-Was. *pr.adj.* 2.
Type of art, theatre, literature, or fashion
associated with the culture.

Balinese puppet show or **shadow
puppet show,** *pr.n.* Ancient form of
theatrical storytelling performed on Earth-
That-Was and throughout the 'Verse. In a
darkened theater, performers attach two-
and three-dimensional figures to sticks.
Then, they guide the puppets' movements
behind a lit screen to act out scenes for
viewers. The show, performers, and
puppets have since adopted other cultural

influences, namely Chinese influences, into
the performance. Mal and Inara attend a
performance to meet Rance Burgess in
"Heart of Gold".

Balls and Bayonet Brigade, *pr.n.*
Nickname of an Independent military unit
that fought in the Unification War. Present
at the decisive Battle of Serenity. Led by
Sergeant Malcolm Reynolds.

bao, *n.* Ancient Chinese dish from Earth-
That-Was. Bun made from leavened
dough. Filled with pork, poultry, or
vegetables, then steamed.

barbed wire, *n.* Wire woven with twisted

strands of wire cut off at short intervals. The protruding wires are sharp and designed to cause damage to humans and animals. Often applied to fences to ward off trespassers and thieves or to contain livestock.

barbed wire whip, *n.* Torture device. Length of barbed wire attached to a long handle. Designed to break the skin when flogging a prisoner. More painful than a leather whip. Used in "War Stories" by the Torturer.

barker, *n.* Person tasked with encouraging visitors to buy tickets or attend a theatrical performance, carnival, or sideshow attraction.

Bathgate Abbey, *pr.n.* Abbey located on Ariel, near Ariel City. Shepherd Book visited Bathgate Abbey during "Ariel".

battle, *n.* 1. Military conflict between two opposing forces, usually armed, that takes place on a field or in space during a war. The battles of the Unification War, like the Battle of Serenity, hold historical weight and are thoroughly documented by the Alliance. Reports of the Unification War battles are part of Alliance propaganda. *n.* 2. Intense fight between two armed

individuals or groups. *adj.* 3. Of wounds or scars. Used in the literal and figurative sense by individuals who participated in a battle or fight. Often, a badge of honor.

Battle of Du-Khang, *pr.n.* Location of a major battle that took place approximately a year before the Battle of Serenity on Hera during the Unification War. Private Tracey Smith, Sergeant Malcolm Reynolds, and Corporal Zoë Alleyne fought in this battle during the winter months along with their unit, the 57th Overlanders. Mal's command of the battle was caused, in part, by the

'In the war to unite the planets, the Battle of Serenity was among the most devastating and decisive. Located on Hera, the valley was considered a key position by both sides, and was bitterly fought over. The Independent Faction, with sixteen brigades and twenty air-tank squads, held the valley against Alliance forces for almost two months, until superior numbers and a deep-flank strategy by General Richard Wilkins led to an Alliance victory.'

– Simon Tam's Universal Encyclopedia, "Serenity"

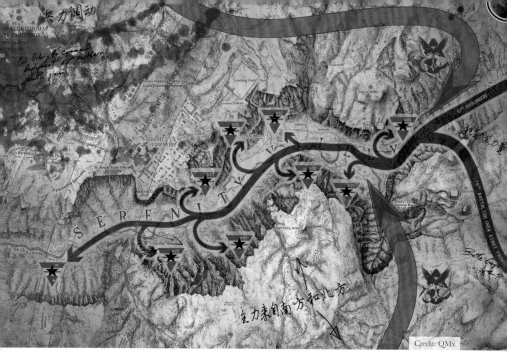

ABOVE: This evocative, bloodstained QMx poster details the Independents' sad defeat at Serenity Valley.
OPPOSITE: Alliance gunships flying overhead to bomb Serenity Valley at the end of the Battle of Serenity.

inexperienced lieutenant on the field who suffered from war-time trauma that put him in a near-catatonic state. After Mal tried to find a fellow Independent officer named Vitelli, he discovered that he'd surrendered to Allied forces which exposed a weakness in their formation, giving the enemy the advantage. Mal opted to abandon their position at the ruins of a Buddhist temple and join forces with the 22nd unit in a school, but just as they were about to leave, the Allied forces attacked, wounding Private Smith in the process. This account was revealed in "The Message".

Battle of Serenity, *pr.n.* Last and decisive battle of the Unification War fought in the year 2511. Took place in Serenity Valley on the planet Hera, which is a Border planet located in the Georgia System. According to Zoë's account in "Serenity", the battle claimed over half a million casualties on both sides. Sergeant Malcolm Reynolds

commanded up to 4,000 troops, but by the end of the battle 400 survivors were left. The surviving troops remained on the battlefield for another seven days while commanders negotiated the peace terms of the Independent Faction's surrender. Over the course of that week, another 250 soldiers died. All that remained of Mal's command, the Balls and Bayonet Brigade, was 151 soldiers, including Corporal Zoë Alleyne. The battle was also a significant turning point for Mal, because he felt betrayed by the outcome. During the fighting, he wore a cross and inspired his troops by sharing his faith. Afterwards, Mal no longer clung to his beliefs and was visibly upset when Shepherd Book boarded *Serenity*.

beacon, *n.* Device used by ships to attract attention. A beacon transmits a signal over a public or private channel to note the position and status of a ship in space.

The listener uses the information to find the source of the signal. These devices are installed on every ship as part of the emergency system. They may also be used as decoys to trick law enforcement and defer attention away from a ship.

"We sent out a beacon. Even managed to boost it a little. Now, if by some chance we do get a response, there's gotta be someone here to answer."
– Captain Malcolm Reynolds, "Out of Gas"

beans, *n. pl.* Canned food favored by military forces. Baked beans have a high nutritional value, are easily packed, and have a long shelf life if unopened. May be eaten hot or cold with a fork, spoon, pair of chopsticks, or spork. Tracey Smith eats beans during the Battle of Du-Khang in "The Message".

Beaumonde, *pr.n.* Planet in the Kalidasa System. It is a destination that the *Serenity* crew headed towards in the beginning of the season, but could never reach due to unforeseen circumstances.

being buzzed, *id.* Refers to a ship being scanned by law enforcement on the lookout for criminals. In the black, Alliance spaceships scan sections of space to search for ships belonging to illegal salvagers or pirates.

Bellerophon, *pr.n.* Planet in the White Sun System and home to the insanely wealthy.

Bellerophon Estates, *pr.n. pl.* Floating, luxury islands owned by the richest billionaires in the 'Verse. Each estate is a self-sustaining paradise and belongs to an Alliance loyalist, like former bio-weapons

expert Durran Haymer. The Estates are located on the planet of Bellerophon. They appeared in the episode "Trash".

belly dancing, *n.* Type of ancient dance performed by women that originated in the Middle East on Earth-That-Was. Belly dancing is a Westernized term describing a dancer who undulates the muscles in her torso. There are many forms of belly dancing, like the style performed by the entertainer who slips Mal a message in "The Train Job".

Bendis, *pr.n.* Solider who fought with Mal and Zoë in the Unification War at the Battle of Serenity.

Bernadette, *pr.n.* White Sun System planet located near Londinium.

Bernoulli, *pr.n.* Client who set up a deal with Captain Reynolds to smuggle Canton

ABOVE: The Bellerophon Estates are home to the super-wealthy on the planet Bellerophon in the Core. Each estate is a self-sustaining island that floats over the ocean. They are an amalgamation of natural comforts and the latest advances in personal security and technology.

LEFT: A belly dancer entertaining patrons in a tavern during "The Train Job".

mud off Higgins' Moon in "Jaynestown".

Bester, *pr.n.* First mechanic who worked on *Serenity*. Kaylee's former lover. He was fired as ship's mechanic when Kaylee proved her intuitive knowledge of ships was greater than his. Referred to in a flashback during "Out of Gas".

Beylix, *pr.n.* Planet in the Kalidasa System. Monty, an Independent veteran, was arrested there. Referenced in "Trash".

bioluminescence, *n.* Light produced by a chemical reaction that occurs in the body of a living organism, typically invertebrates, insects, and bacteria.

bioluminescent, *adj.* Of the natural light a bio-organism, like a firefly or algae, emits. May also refer to a body of water that reflects the light caused by this phenomenon. A biolumniescent lake may be found on Ariel.

biowarfare or **germ warfare,** *n.* Use of synthetic or natural toxins and infectious agents designed to kill or seriously injure large numbers of soldiers or civilians.

bio-weapon, *n.* 1. Device engineered to deploy gases or spores to devastate entire populations as part of biowarfare. *adj.* 2. Of a device or person whose purpose is to engage in biowarfare.

"Haymer's Alliance. Bio-weapons expert during the war. He'd target neighborhoods with valuables, wipe out every living soul without ever damaging the goods. Go in, take whatever he wanted."

– Saffron, "Trash"

bird, *n. sl.* Spaceship.

birddoggin', *v. sl.* 1. Stealing. *v. sl.* 2. Crossing through an area illegally.

birthday, *n.* Celebration marking the day a human was born. Simon Tam celebrates his birthday with the *Serenity* crew at the beginning of "Out of Gas".

bit, *n. sl.* Smallest unit of currency. Least valuable. Coin.

black, the, *n. sl.* Remote area of space far from civilization where few celestial bodies can be seen.

black mark, *n.* Notation next to a client's name in the client registry. Lifelong ban that prohibits the individual from requesting a Companion's services or visiting a House. A black mark is given when the client abuses a Companion. It's the Companion's right to decide whether or not the client has earned the black mark according to Guild Law. Inara Serra gives Atherton Wing a black mark at the conclusion of "Shindig".

black market, *n.* 1. General term describing the illicit trade performed by smugglers, thieves, crime bosses, salvagers, and opportunists who sell, trade, or traffic unsanctioned goods. The rules governing trade in the 'Verse are strict and fall under the purview of an Alliance-run Guild, which is also referred to as the Trader's Guild. Buyers, sellers, and salvagers must request permits and have proper paperwork on hand, or risk being arrested. As a result, the black market is omnipresent, especially outside the Core. A black market is not identified as such based on the inherent worth or value of the goods traded. Derelict salvage operations performed without a permit and human trafficking, for example, are both punishable by law to varying degrees. Illicit commodities bought, salvaged, smuggled, and sold in the *Firefly* TV show include: crates of supplies for government settlers, medicine, wobbly-headed geisha dolls, the Lassiter, slaves, cattle, Canton mud, and blastomeres. *n.* 2. Physical location where commodities are bought, sold, and traded illegally. To avoid detection, black markets tend to be set up in a temporary space that can be abandoned quickly. Monty set up a temporary black market in "Trash" on an uninhabited moon. He transported goods in his freighter, then displayed them for fellow smugglers nearby.

blackberry, *n.* Type of dark, bulbous fruit that grows on a bush. In the original script for "Safe", Simon and River recalled happy memories of eating blackberries.

blackout zone, *n.* Area where electrical and radio transmissions are disrupted, and access to the Cortex is either limited or nonexistent. Government officials and law enforcement are unable to effectively monitor and patrol that location which, in turn, encourages criminal and traitorous activity. As such, the areas are deemed hazardous to the public's safety, and it is illegal to be found in a blackout zone. Simon Tam sought help from a blackout-zone coalition to free his sister on Osiris.

blastomere, *n.* Highly illegal, bio-

ABOVE: Mal and Saffron meet at a black market exchange run by Monty, and plan to steal the Lassiter in order to sell it for millions of credits on the black market.

ABOVE: Tracey Smith, who fought with Zoë and Mal in the Unification War, attempts to smuggle highly illegal blastomeres in "The Message". His attempt to bait the *Serenity* crew into helping him ended in disaster.

engineered organ attached inside a living host until it matures to full growth. If the blastomere is not extracted in time, the host dies. Blastomeres are high tech and extremely valuable on the black market. Tracey Smith was carrying blastomeres inside his torso in "The Message" and was supposed to have them removed on Ariel. This did not happen according to plan.

ZOË: You're smuggling human organs?

TRACEY: But not from a person. I wouldn't do a thing like that. Grown in a lab. Only way they can be moved is in a person. Not sure why.

SIMON: Because the technology's not ready. The blastomeres are unapproved. Likely unstable. You're not just a carrier – you're an incubator.

– "The Message"

ABOVE: The Blue Sun Corporation logo is ubiquitous in the 'Verse. It appears in advertisements and on goods, like this commercial on a public vidphone in "Ariel", and Jayne Cobb's T-shirt.

Bloggs, Joey, *pr.n.* Name supplied to Malcolm Reynolds by Adelai Niska during "The Train Job" to cover the real reason he was visiting the planet Regina. Unbeknownst to Mal, Joey Bloggs had already shot himself and died.

blowback, *n.* 1. Unintended, negative side effect that occurs as a result of overtaxing a ship's engines while still in an atmosphere. Blowback damages the ship and shuts down the engines. *n.* 2. Unforeseen consequences that occur after acting or speaking. Usually related to a controversial or morally questionable issue.

blubber, *v. sl.* 1. Derogatory way to describe the act of crying. *n.* 2. Human or whale fat.

blubberous, *adj. sl.* Insult referring to an obese person. As big as a whale. Saffron recalls seeing other girls on her planet being married off to unappealingly blubberous men. She is resultingly delighted to have been promised to the rather more attractive Malcolm Reynolds.

Blue Sun Corporation, *pr.n.* Mega-corporation responsible for the manufacturing of goods and services ranging from food and medicine to textiles and appliances. The Blue Sun Corporation is omnipresent throughout the 'Verse, and its logo can be found everywhere on items ranging from canned food and coffee to T-shirts and ships. The mega-corporation is a multi-faceted entity that means different things to different people.

To most, Blue Sun Corp. presents itself as an asset to humanity that focuses on selling the necessities of life. To members of parliament and Alliance politicians, on the other hand, Blue Sun Corp. is a government contractor and ally that has "donated" large sums of money to protect and further its interests. To its corporate rivals, it is a dangerous enemy that will not stop at murder to glean secrets from the competition. To its surviving victims, Blue Sun Corp. is a sinister and nigh unbeatable foe that has no ethics or morals. River Tam slashes Jayne Cobb with a knife across his T-shirt's Blue Sun logo in "Ariel".

Blue Sun System, *pr.n.* Newest terraformed planetary system in the 'Verse. Part of the rim. Deadwood is a planet in the Blue Sun System.

boat, *n. fem.* 1. Vessel used to travel on water. *n. sl.* 2. Spaceship. All ships are referred to as "she", and take on "feminine" characteristics.

body bag, *n.* Aluminum, coffin-like case that contains the body of a corpse. Used in "Ariel" to transport Simon and River Tam into St Lucy's Medical Center.

Bolles, *pr.n.* Middleman who was making a deal with Mal when he got shot in "War Stories". Prior to his death, Bolles was to receive and sell the medicine the crew stole from St Lucy's Medical Center on Ariel.

bone-tired, *adj. sl.* Completely exhausted. Ready to fall over. Extremely worn down.

Shepherd Derrial Book

*"You don't fix faith, River.
It fixes you."*

— "Jaynestown"

The enigmatic Shepherd from Southdown Abbey speaks clearly, with authority, and swears the least of any character on the show. The clues to unlocking Shepherd Book's past lie in his dialogue, which is more similar to Simon's and Inara's way of speaking than to that of the other characters who grew up outside the Core. When the Shepherd is tending to his flock, he'll maintain his composure to act as both spiritual guide and counselor and his speech reflects this. Book tends to avoid using contractions or familiar turns of phrase. Instead, his natural way of speaking often incorporates proper grammatical usage, befitting someone who is well educated from the Core. On occasion, however, a few words will slip into his vocabulary that reflect more casual speech patterns such as: "heathens a-plenty", "mite fuzzier", or "'Fraid I might be needin' a preacher".

Shepherd Book favors the use of the word "son" and will use proper titles when referring to people in positions of power such as "Commander" or "Captain". Book's anecdotes often tie in to his beliefs, and many of the character's memorable lines broach the subject of his faith in some fashion. Unlike the other characters, Book rarely speaks in Chinese and only swore once on the show – after seeing what Niska did to Mal in "War Stories".

Shepherd-speak:

"I brought you some supper. But if you'd prefer a lecture, I've a few very catchy ones prepared. Sin and hellfire. One has lepers."

bonnet, *n.* Type of hat sewn from plain or printed fabric that ties under the chin, either with a ribbon, string, or two narrow pieces of material that extend from the front of the hat. While there are many styles of bonnets worn by men and women, Mal wears a floral prairie bonnet designed for traveling across long distances in "Our Mrs Reynolds". The prairie bonnet is a popular choice among settlers, because it can be used to frame and hide the wearer's face, shielding it from the elements.

booby trap, *n.* Device or mechanical system that results in the injury, capture, or death of a person or animal. May also be devised to force the destruction of property. Most booby traps are designed with a trigger mechanism that must be pressed or released to activate the trap. The devices range in size and may incorporate a lure of some kind. Reavers attach booby traps to ships they've attacked, in order to maximize the damage they can cause.

MAL: It's a real burden being right so often.
WASH: What is it?
MAL: Booby trap. Reavers sometimes leave 'em behind for the rescue ships. We triggered it when we latched on.
WASH: And when we detach –
MAL: – it blows.
– "Bushwhacked"

Book, Shepherd Derrial, *pr.n.* Preacher with a mysterious past from Southdown Abbey who joins the *Serenity* crew in "Serenity" as a passenger. One of the nine

LEFT AND ABOVE: Shepherd Book takes up arms for his captain in "War Stories" (left) and spots a fed station on the control panel display in "The Message" (above).

primary crewmembers. He is shot during "Safe". When the Captain approaches an Alliance cruiser for help, it's revealed that Shepherd Book has a secret past that affords him clearance with the Alliance.

booty, *n.* Stolen loot. Goods to be smuggled. A throwback reference to pirate treasure.

Border planets, *pr.n. pl.* Celestial bodies within the Georgia and Red Sun Systems. This area of the 'Verse surrounds the Core and is considered part of the frontier. In a post-Unification War environment, the Border planets are still rebuilding after the devastation, and work is hard to come by. Here, it is not uncommon to find isolated settlements founded upon a religious belief, like the Triumph Settlement, or the town the Patron oversees on Jiangyin, nor is it unusual to find indentured servants or slaves, like the Mudders who work for Magistrate Higgins. The Border planets are patrolled by Alliance cruisers and, because their municipalities aren't anywhere near as sophisticated as those in the Core, folk rely on the government for subsidies or for medicine to counteract the effects of illness caused by terraforming.

Boros, *pr.n.* Planet in the Georgia System. Several Alliance colonies have taken root on Boros; the Alliance's military presence is also strong here. Referenced in "Serenity".

bound by law, *id.* To be arrested by law enforcement, charged with crimes, and judged accordingly. The phrase is spoken by officers of the law before a citizen is arrested. When a suspect is bound by law and ordered to stand down, the officer expects that person to comply.

bounty, *n.* Reward for capturing and returning a specific person to an interested party. In order to earn the reward, the terms of the capture must be fulfilled. Usually, the gift awarded is a generous financial sum. Used interchangeably with the word "reward".

bountyhunter, *n.* Person who searches for fugitives in order to collect a reward.

Typically, a bountyhunter does not get paid until the terms of a bounty are fulfilled. Jubal Early was a bountyhunter who tracked River down in "Objects in Space".

Bourne, Sheriff, *pr.n.* Officer of the law in charge of investigating crimes for the town of Paradiso on the planet Regina in the Georgia System. Sheriff Bourne is a practical man who places an emphasis on dealing with the problem at hand. He is willing to let a crime slide in order to protect the people of his town. Sheriff Bourne appeared in "The Train Job" and was the chief investigator in charge of discovering what happened to the crates of medicine stolen from the Alliance-occupied train.

SHERIFF BOURNE: You were truthful back in town. These are tough times. Hard to find yourself work. A man can get a job, he might not look too close at what that job is. (To Mal.) But a man learns all the details of a situation like ours, well then he has a choice.

MAL: I don't believe he does.

– "The Train Job"

Bowden's Malady, *pr.n.* 1. Degenerative disease that afflicts bone and muscle. *pr.n.* 2. Localized illness contracted by settlers who live in Paradiso on the planet Regina. The town's original miners contracted the disease as a result of the terraforming process and passed it on to their children. New workers will eventually suffer from the illness as well. It is treatable with a medicine called Pescaline D.

Bowie, *pr.n.* 1. Weapons manufacturer. *pr.adj.* 2. Type of knife. Often used by soldiers and mercenaries, like Jayne Cobb, and worn on the belt in a case.

brainblown, *adj. sl.* Refers to death by a shot to the head. A blast so powerful that it blows a person's brains from their skull.

brainpan, *n. sl.* Skull.

brass, *n. sl.* Ranking military commanders

or government leaders responsible for making the important decisions, e.g. "I hear top brass made this call."

Breed, *pr.n.* Corbin's right-hand man and Saffron's third partner who runs a Carrion House. Appears in "Our Mrs Reynolds".

bridge, *n.* 1. Structure built to allow passage over a body of water, ravine, or other obstacle. *n.* 2. Raised area, platform, or room on a spaceship where the captain issues commands to personnel. The

dimensions of the bridge often correspond to the ship's class and size. On *Serenity*, for example, the bridge is small and located past the foredeck. On the *I.A.V. Dortmunder*, the bridge is a large room filled with personnel and monitors.

Bridget, *pr.n.* Saffron's alias when marrying Monty. Her ruse was exposed in "Trash".

brig, *n.* Holding cell located on a ship, e.g. "Should we throw 'em in the brig, cap'n?"

bris, *n. masc.* 1. Jewish ritual performed to

BELOW: Mal and Wash at the control panel as they assess the situation on *Serenity*'s bridge.

LEFT: A close-up of the bridge's control panel. Some of its design details take inspiration from Chinese coins.

Vitelli's out of it. That bumblebee laid down arms at the first sign of inevitable crushing defeat. Can you imagine such a cowardly creature?" – Sergeant Malcolm Reynolds, "The Message"

circumcise males on Earth-that-Was. *n. masc. sl.* 2. The opposite of an extended period of torture resulting in great pain and torment. A careful, small cut performed quickly to avoid inflicting any pain.

Browncoat, *pr.n.* 1. Nickname for a member of the Independent Faction who fought against the Anglo-Sino Alliance in the Unification War. Following the war, Browncoats scattered all across the 'Verse. Many veterans have rejected Alliance rule and eke out a meager living as smugglers and illegal salvagers operating on the Border planets or rim. *n. lc.* 2. Style of leather longcoat that fuses Western and Eastern influences. Worn by Mal Reynolds.

brute, *n. masc.* 1. Man with an imposing or threatening physical appearance. *n.* 2. Person who is harsh, crude, and insensitive, e.g. "Jayne Cobb is such a brute!" *adj.* 3. Extremely strong, e.g. "They smashed through our barricade with brute force."

Brutus, *pr.n.* A ship Shepherd Book was considering traveling on in "Serenity".

Buhnder, *pr.n.* Firearms manufacturer. A Buhnder gun was referenced by Jayne in "The Message".

bulkhead, *n.* Ship's partition or wall designed to protect crewmembers in the event of an emergency, like a fire or leak.

bullet-grabber, *n.* Surgical tool designed to grip and safely remove a bullet. Simon Tam has a bullet-grabber in his medical kit.

bumblebee, *n. sl.* Person who's behaving like an insect. Useless. Insignificant.

bunk, *n.* 1. Crewmember's quarters on a ship. *n.* 2. Narrow, small bed.

Burgess, Belinda, *pr.n.* Socialite and wife of Rance Burgess who lives on Deadwood. Belinda is unable to bear children. She appeared in "Heart of Gold".

(Burgess), Jonah, *pr.n.* Name of the child born to Petaline in "Heart of Gold". Jonah was confirmed as Rance's illegitimate son.

Burgess, Rance, *pr.n.* Self-appointed ruler on Deadwood. Rance pays an Alliance dignitary bribes to get his hands on advanced technology, which he uses to throw his weight around. Rance was the reason why the *Serenity* crew visited Deadwood, as he was obsessed with kidnapping his illegitimate son from a prostitute named Petaline.

busker, *n.* Street or public performer. Typically paid by donations. May entertain by singing, dancing, playing an instrument, or performing theatrics.

by the head, *id.* Method of assigning costs per unit where one unit equals one cow's head. Mal was to receive thirty a head for the cattle he delivered in "Safe".

bygones, *n. pl.* Moments that occurred previously. Historic or former events. *adj.* 2. Of the distant past.

bypass system, *n.* On a ship, a series of wires and parts that redirect the flow of a more complex network, to speed up the original system's processes and functionality.

byphodine, *n.* Drug that makes a patient appear dead to the untrained eye.

LEFT: The browncoat and other brown clothing signify Independent Faction soldiers. Mal and Zoë fought on the side of the Independents during the Unification War.

Cabott, *pr.n.* Socialite and friend of Banning Miller in "Shindig".

Cadrie Pond, *pr.n.* Located on Persephone, the area where the duel between Malcolm Reynolds and Atherton Wing took place in "Shindig".

Callahan, *pr.n.* Manufacturer name for rifles and guns. Jayne's rifle, Vera, is a Callahan model.

"Six men came to kill me one time, and the best of them carried this. It's a Callahan fullbore autolock, customized trigger and double cartridge thorough-gauge. "
– Jayne Cobb, "Our Mrs Reynolds"

Cambersons' estate, *pr.n.* The Tam family's neighbor. The Cambersons live on Osiris and grow hodgeberries on their land. Referenced by Simon in "Safe".

cannibalism, *n.* Act of consuming the flesh and organs of one's own species. It is considered taboo and a sign of mental illness or brain damage. Reavers, who are regarded as mindless space zombies or rage-propelled berzerkers, eat the living or dead flesh of their victims.

Canton, *pr.n.* Town located on Higgins' Moon. The location of Canton Mudworks. Canton's mud bogs emit a foul odor. The episode "Jaynestown" took place here.

SIMON: Canton really stinks.

MAL: That's what makes it such a great drop point. No one comes here that doesn't have to.

WASH: I vote we do this job really, really fast.
– "Jaynestown"

Canton Mudworks, *pr.n.* Business whose main purpose is to collect and ship mud to clients throughout the 'Verse. The unique chemical composition of the mud turned this everyday commodity into a highly sought-after resource. Canton Mudworks is owned by Magistrate Higgins and run by a foreman and his prods. The company employs indentured servants who are paid a pittance in exchange for their labor. Canton Mudworks is located on Higgins' Moon. It appears in "Jaynestown".

Canton riot, *pr.n.* Labor uprising on Higgins' Moon. Following the perceived gift from Jayne Cobb, the Mudders took it upon themselves to demand that their boss, Magistrate Higgins, provide them with better working conditions.

Canton whiskey, *pr.n.* Cheap spirit made, bottled, and sold in Canton.

Capital City, *pr.n.* Name of a metropolis found on the planet Osiris in the White Sun System.

ABOVE: Mudders excavating mud at Canton Mudworks. The *Serenity* crew inspects their work.

RIGHT: Map given to cast and crew to help orient them while filming "Jaynestown" at Sable Ranch, which was used as the location of Canton.

Credit:
Danny Nero

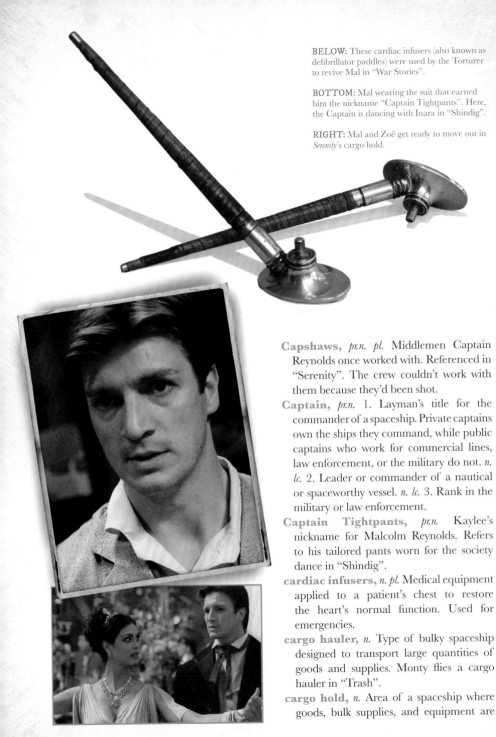

BELOW: These cardiac infusers (also known as defibrillator paddles) were used by the Torturer to revive Mal in "War Stories".

BOTTOM: Mal wearing the suit that earned him the nickname "Captain Tightpants". Here, the Captain is dancing with Inara in "Shindig".

RIGHT: Mal and Zoë get ready to move out in *Serenity*'s cargo hold.

Capshaws, *pr.n. pl.* Middlemen Captain Reynolds once worked with. Referenced in "Serenity". The crew couldn't work with them because they'd been shot.

Captain, *pr.n.* 1. Layman's title for the commander of a spaceship. Private captains own the ships they command, while public captains who work for commercial lines, law enforcement, or the military do not. *n. lc.* 2. Leader or commander of a nautical or spaceworthy vessel. *n. lc.* 3. Rank in the military or law enforcement.

Captain Tightpants, *pr.n.* Kaylee's nickname for Malcolm Reynolds. Refers to his tailored pants worn for the society dance in "Shindig".

cardiac infusers, *n. pl.* Medical equipment applied to a patient's chest to restore the heart's normal function. Used for emergencies.

cargo hauler, *n.* Type of bulky spaceship designed to transport large quantities of goods and supplies. Monty flies a cargo hauler in "Trash".

cargo hold, *n.* Area of a spaceship where goods, bulk supplies, and equipment are

stored. Smugglers tend to modify their cargo holds by building false panels and hidden nooks to store illicit goods.

Carrion House, *pr.n.* Type of illegal salvage operation that preys upon ships and ship parts for their financial value. A Carrion House is run by hijackers who target potential ships elsewhere in the black. In many cases, the ships at that time are fully functional. First, a con artist deceives and disables a crew from responding. Then, the con artist heads straight for the cockpit to sabotage the flight controls and reprogram the ship's trajectory. This automated flight path guides the ship into an electromagnetic net where it's trapped and unable to break free. If the ship is still occupied at that point, the passengers are usually killed. Then, the ships are either sold intact on the black market or stripped for parts. In "Our Mrs Reynolds", Saffron plays the role of the con artist working for the Carrion House alongside her partners.

carvings, *n. pl.* Type of souvenir. On Jiangyin in "Safe", the carvings were wooden ducks.

catalyzer, *n.* Part of a system that turns the primary engine in a spaceship to generate power. The catalyzer is a piece of the compression coil. It is a part that, when broken, cannot be repaired.

KAYLEE: Catalyzer on the port compression coil blew. That's where the trouble started.
MAL: I need that in dummy talk, Kaylee.
KAYLEE: We're dead in the water.
– "Out of Gas"

cattle, *n.* In the 'Verse, cows and bulls are a commodity like any other. There are rules governing their transport and sale according to Guild Law. Unique brands or contracts may reflect ownership. The cattle Mal transports from Persephone ("Shindig") to Jiangyin ("Safe") were sold illegally.

catwalk, *n.* A narrow platform, bridge, or walkway. On *Serenity*, the catwalk runs throughout the ship. For example, the bridge overlooking the cargo bay is part of the catwalk. This part of the walkway is accessible from stairwells located on both

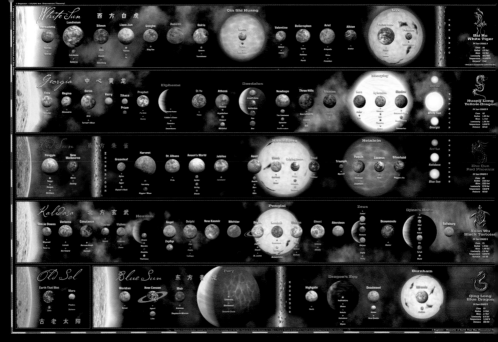

Credit: QMx

"After the Earth was used up, we found a new solar system and hundreds of new Earths were terraformed and colonized. The Central planets formed the Alliance and decided all the planets had to join under their rule. There was some disagreement on that point. After the War, many of the Independents who had fought and lost drifted to the edges of the system, far from Alliance control. Out here, people struggled to get by with the most basic technologies; a ship would bring you work, a gun would help you keep it. A captain's goal was simple: find a crew, find a job, keep flying."

— Shepherd Book, opening monologue

sides of the cargo bay. A door allows the crew to enter the main part of the ship.

central, *adj.* 1. Of, at, or forming the middle. *pr.adj. uc.* 2. Of the Core, the seat of human civilization. When used, the description infers a tie to the Alliance, e.g. "I can't believe you called Central Transport again. They won't fly us to Jiangyin."

Central Authority, *pr.n.* Name referring to a legal governing body of the Anglo-Sino Alliance. The Central Authority is located on Londinium in the White Sun System. It is the twenty-sixth-century equivalent of the F.B.I., C.I.A., and N.S.A.

Central planets, *pr.n.* The center of the known 'Verse and the seat of human civilization. Refers to planets and moons within the White Sun System including Ariel, Londinium, Sihnon, Persephone, Santo, Bellerophon, Osiris, and others.

ceramic, *n.* 1. Hard solid made from clay mixed with another inorganic material that's then fired. *adj.* 2. Of an object made out of this material. *n. pl.* 3. General term for objects formed from this material. Used widely for everything from dishes to ship parts.

chain of command, *n.* Group of people organized into a hierarchy based on power level. In the military, the chain of command is based on rank. On smaller ships, even though the captain is in command, subordinate positions are assigned based on need or personality traits. For example, Zoë Alleyne Washburne is Captain Reynolds' first mate. If the Captain is unavailable to lead, then Zoë takes over like she did in "War Stories".

Chari, *pr.n.* Prostitute at the Heart of Gold who turns traitorous and allies herself with Rance Burgess, acting as a double-agent. She's partly to blame for the attack on the brothel to retrieve Burgess's son.

Chinese, *pr.n.* 1. Refers to a linguistic family spoken on Earth-That-Was in China and its surrounding countries. Chinese contains many dialects and languages, including Mandarin and Cantonese. *pr.n.* 2. Refers to people who ethnically identify as Chinese based on their heritage and ability to trace their roots back to Earth-That-Was. *pr.adj.* 3. Of the Chinese culture. May refer to the culture from the distant past back on Earth-That-Was, or the culture that exists

OPPOSITE: QMx's double-sided Map of the 'Verse, which was two years in the making, details the White Sun System (aka the Central planets) as part of the wider 'Verse. This system is the home of the Alliance.

BELOW: View of Ariel City's skyline from the municipal junkyard, as seen in "Ariel".

at the time of the twenty-sixth century.

Chinese Checkers, *pr.n.* Board game for two to six players. The board, which is usually made of wood, has a series of indentations that form a six-pointed star. Colored marbles are placed into the points of the star, and each participating player commands a unique color. The object of the game is to move the marbles from their original position on the board to the exact opposite side. On a player's turn, a marble may be moved to the nearest indentation, or may "jump" over another marble to an empty spot. The winner of the game is the player who accomplishes the objective the fastest. The *Serenity* crew plays a game of Chinese Checkers at the beginning of "The Train Job" in a bar.

❖ To learn more about the Chinese language, turn to pp. 136-55. There, you'll read an interview with *Firefly* TV translator Jenny Lynn and find the Chinese words and phrases from the show.

---

chin-wig, *n. masc. sl.* Wild or unruly goatee or beard.

chop shop, *n. sl.* Illegal salvage operation run by thieves who steal vehicles to strip them for their parts and then sell them on the black market. Commonly, chop shops are located in remote locations in the black to decrease their chances of being detected by the feds.

chopsticks, *n. pl.* Ancient utensils used to eat solid food. A reusable pair of thin sticks, usually carved out of wood, that are painted or polished. Commonly used by people who originated from eastern Asia back on Earth-That-Was. In the 'Verse, chopsticks have replaced forks and knives as the preferred eating utensils. Hot liquids, like soups, are eaten with a spoon.

Chore Poker, *pr.n.* Title of the game that the *Serenity* crew plays to bet chores instead of chips or money. Played in "Shindig".

The actual variant of poker is called "Tall Card".

Christmas, *pr.n.* 1. Ancient holiday that survived the passage from Earth-That-Was to the 'Verse. Though it is still celebrated, cultural and religious traditions vary widely depending upon planetary or lunar customs. *pr.n.* 2. In its negative connotation, referred to sarcastically to reflect a nasty surprise or string of bad luck.

MAL: Is it Christmas?
ZOË: Yes, sir, it's Christmas. That special night when Nick the Saint comes down your chimney, changes your course, blows out the navcom, seals the bridge and takes off in your shuttle.
– "Our Mrs Reynolds"

clay, *n.* 1. Fine-grained, wet soil composed of minerals, which has the properties of soft plastic. Clay comes in many colors, and may be white, grey, brown, black, orange, or red. *n.* 2. Prized commodity collected and sold at Canton Mudworks on Higgins' Moon.

click, *n.* Unit of measurement commonly used in space. Roughly, one click is equal to half a mile.

client registry, *n.* Database of all clients who have used the services of a Companion. In order to become a client, a citizen must register with a desired Companion or House.

Cobb, Jayne, *pr.n.* Crude mercenary motivated by money. In exchange for his muscle, he's granted room and board on *Serenity* and part of the take for each job. He consistently butts heads with the Captain. After a series of confrontations and events, like the sacrifice of Meadows in "Jaynestown", he softens, only to "get stupid" whenever money is flashed in front of him.

Cobb, Mama, *pr.n.* Jayne Cobb's mother. She mails him an orange, knit hat as a

Jayne Cobb

Jayne Cobb is a vulgar mercenary whose dialogue reflects his lack of education, his life outside the Core, and his criminal background. Like Zoë, he won't give long speeches and, as shown in "Jaynestown", will feel uncomfortable if forced to speak at length. He's the gruffest crewmember on board *Serenity* and will say the first (inappropriate) words that come to mind, which often results in either a reprimand from Mal or hurting someone else's feelings. His dialogue is a mixture of slang, creative grammatical usage, and dropped letters or alternate spellings of words.

Serenity's muscle prefers to use words like "gonna", "ya", "'em", and "crap-heel" along with dropping the "g" for words ending in -ing such as "jumpin'" and "stickin'". Jayne's sentences are often truncated and he'll defer to slang or colloquialisms instead of sounding out every syllable. For example, the mercenary would say "Don't make no sense" or "How come they ain't blowin' us out of the air?"

Jayne won't hesitate to swear (whether it's appropriate or not), and his Chinese words and phrases reflect this aspect of his character.

Jayne-speak:

"Can't get paid if you crawl away like a bitty little bug, neither."

"You don't pay me to talk pretty."

"I'll be in my bunk."

— "War Stories"

"I got a few letters at first, then I didn't hear for months. Finally, I got a letter that made no sense. She talked about things that never happened, jokes we never ... it was code. I couldn't even figure ... I talked to professors, spent a week trying to work it out. It just said ... They're hurting us. Get me out. " – Simon Tam, "Serenity"

thank you for sending home credits in "The Message".

Cobb, Matty, *pr.n.* Jayne Cobb's younger relative who is suffering from a lung disease. Jayne sends home part of his take to cover Matty's medical expenses.

cockpit, *n.* Area where the pilot sits at the controls of a spaceship. In most non-commercial, medium-sized vessels, the cockpit is a small area that can be closed off. In larger ships, like an Alliance cruiser, the cockpit is integrated into the bridge's design, and the bridge itself may be closed off via one or two doors. For some military spacecraft or emergency shuttles, access to the cockpit is not shut off due to space limitations.

code, *n.* 1. Cipher designed to transmit information or authorized commands between two people belonging to the same military force or organization. *n.* 2. Secret system based on a particular language designed to hide a message. Cryptograms may be entirely invented or based on an existing method to encrypt data, like a substitution cipher where letters are swapped with one another. Simon Tam believed that his sister River created a code embedded in the letters she sent to him. This eventually led to her rescue.

cods, *n. pl. masc. vul.* Testicles. From Middle English usage, meaning scrotum.

colonist, *n.* Pioneer who lives in or settles a colony. In most cases, a colonist is an Alliance loyalist from the Central planets who believes, at first, that the act of colonization is a citizen's patriotic duty. If the passage to a colony or the outlook of a settlement meets disaster, however, the colonists' attitudes toward the Alliance shift to an unfavorable position that may result in desertion.

colony, *n.* Group of patriotic people encouraged by the Alliance to leave the Central planets in order to develop a settlement. The foundation of colonies is an attractive political tool used by the Alliance to extend their influence outside the Core. Sanctioned colonies are subject to the same laws that govern citizens who live in the White Sun System, but do not have the direct access to similar resources, amenities, or opportunities that the Core citizens do. To support colonization, the Alliance provides its citizens with subsidies that include genetically-engineered seed, protein bars, medical supplies, and proper authorizations. Despite the Alliance's efforts to recruit interested citizens, however, many colonies fail due to a number of factors ranging from harsh living conditions to starvation and crime.

com, *n. abbr.* Short for communications device. The com allows a ship's captain to

COCKPIT

FORE PASSAGE

STAIRS DOWN TO CARGO BAY

DINING AREA

AFT PASSAGE

STAIRS DOWN TO INFIRMARY

ENGINE ROOM

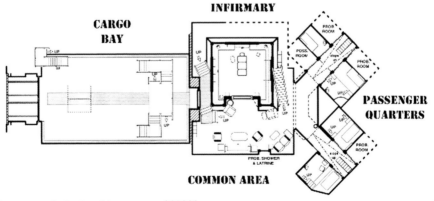

CARGO BAY

INFIRMARY

PROB. ROOM

PDSS. ROOM

PROB. ROOM

PASSENGER QUARTERS

PROB. ROOM

PROB. SHOWER & LATRINE

COMMON AREA

ABOVE: Blueprints for *Serenity* and the cockpit of Inara's shuttle.

broadcast a message to all crewmembers and passengers on board.

Command, *pr.n.* 1. Leaders of the Independent Faction during the Unification War. *v. lc.* 2. To order in an official or forceful fashion according to a level of authority.

Commander, *pr.n.* Title referring to an Alliance military position. A commander, like Commander Harken, takes the helm of an Alliance cruiser to issue commands related to personnel and ship functions. As an official representation of the Alliance, a commander is also responsible for investigating disturbances and making judgment calls that best fit the Alliance's interests.

communication channel, *n.* Designated data-transmission route between a point of origin and a receiver via the Cortex. Communication channels may be public or private, legal or illegal.

Companion, 1. *pr.n.* Twenty-sixth-century equivalent of a French courtesan or a Japanese geisha. A Companion is a government-sanctioned courtesan and, as such, enjoys a high-ranking social status and is well respected. Companions in the Core are selected to live in a House during their youth and study at an Academy before achieving their legal status. Companions who hail from the Border or rim may be older and are brought to a House located in the Central planets. Though sex is a component of their services and considered a sacred union between two souls, all Companions are required to learn a number of different customs and earn high marks in academic fields that include: psychology, linguistics, music, art, theatre, fencing, world cultures, biology, human anatomy, etc. Because a Companion is trained to exude an aura of mystery, rumors often swirl in their wake. For example, it is widely believed that a Companion cannot abandon his/her profession and remain in the Central

planets. While most Companions are female, some male Companions do exist. Inara Serra is an example of a Registered Companion in good standing with the Guild. Former Companions include Nandi and Saffron. *pr.adj.* 2. Of or pertaining to the role of a Companion.

Companion Greeting Ceremony, *pr.n.* Ritual pouring and preparation of tea to welcome a new client during a first meeting as a sign of respect. The Companion Greeting Ceremony is considered a sacred art form and has roots in the Japanese tea ceremony performed on Earth-That-Was.

Companion immunization package, *pr.n.* Medical supply kit. Due to a Companion's social standing, the Alliance provides all Companions with a standardized selection of drugs and medicine for their personal use. The precise contents of the vials are unknown.

Companion license, *pr.n.* Certificate reflecting a Companion's legal status. The license is renewed on an annual basis following a mandatory physical examination. Companions who perform services with an expired license, like entertaining clients, may be arrested and prosecuted.

Companion Registration, *pr.n.* Legal documents filed to grant the required authorization for a potential or existing Companion to provide services for clients. Paperwork includes a Companion's license, medical history, academic record, and other forms of documentation. Companions keep a copy of their license and Registration on hand and may present these documents to law enforcement or officials upon request. Inara Serra shows her Companion Registration to Sheriff Bourne in "The Train Job".

compression coil, *n.* Complex ship part attached to the engine. The compression

"A Companion chooses her own clients; that's Guild Law. But physical appearance doesn't matter so terribly. You look for compatibility of spirit ... there's an energy about a person that's difficult to hide, you try to feel that..."

– Inara Serra, "The Train Job"

ABOVE AND LEFT: Inara's official Companion papers. Companions train in psychology, music, fencing, languages, and unarmed martial arts and must submit to an annual physical exam to maintain their license.

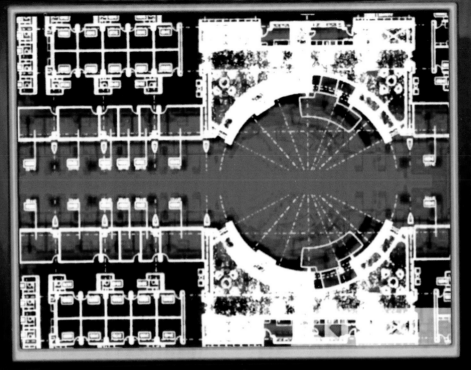

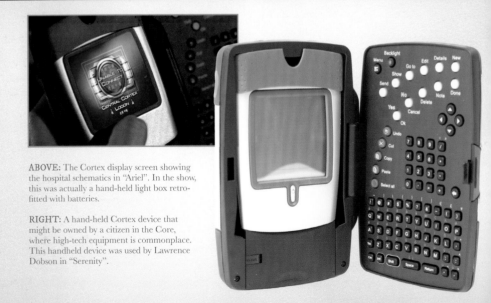

ABOVE: The Cortex display screen showing the hospital schematics in "Ariel". In the show, this was actually a hand-held light box retrofitted with batteries.

RIGHT: A hand-held Cortex device that might be owned by a citizen in the Core, where high-tech equipment is commonplace. This handheld device was used by Lawrence Dobson in "Serenity".

coil is a piece of the system designed to turn an engine to generate power. In a Firefly-class ship, the engine has two compression coils on either side of it which are part of the steamer. Each coil contains a crucial part called a "catalyzer". The poor condition of the *Serenity* compression coil is initially a bone of contention between Captain Reynolds and Kaylee, which eventually results in tragedy during "Out of Gas".

KAYLEE: I'd sure love to find a brand new compression coil for the steamer.

MAL: And I'd like to be king of all Londinium and wear a shiny hat. Just get us some passengers. Them as can pay, all right?

KAYLEE: Compression coil busts, we're drifting ...

MAL: Best not bust, then.

– "Serenity"

conductor cap, *n.* Thick casing designed to stop an electric or electromagnetic output resulting from an accidental or intentional discharge. When applied to a port, outlet, or live cables, the conductor cap prevents a current from being emitted through that conductor. The cap has a number of safety and engineering applications. In "Our Mrs Reynolds", Kaylee regrets not having a conductor cap to help them break free of the Carrion House's net.

console, *n.* Access panel granting a user the ability to program, maintain, monitor, or control a system, object, or vehicle, like a ship. Most ship's consoles are located in the cockpit or on the bridge. For example, the consoles on the bridge of an Alliance cruiser are specialized and require properly trained individuals to operate them.

converted, *adj.* Marks a piece of equipment or a ship that has been modified from its original purpose or shape into something new, e.g. "a converted cargo hauler".

cooling drive, *n.* Ship's system that lowers the temperature of the engines to prevent them from overheating.

Corbin, *pr.n.* Illegal salvager who runs a chop shop in "Our Mrs Reynolds".

The parts are crap ... but you put 'em together, you got a Firefly. Thing will run forever, they got a mechanic even half awake."

– Corbin, "Our Mrs Reynolds"

Core, the, *n. sl.* Another name for the White Sun System and Central planets. The Core refers to the fact that this area of the 'Verse is both the seat of civilization and its governing body, the Alliance.

core containment, *n.* Primary ship's system engineered to prevent the effects of radiation from harming a crew. Reavers fly ships without a core containment system. Knowledge of this trait gives targeted victims the opportunity to detect nearby Reaver ships and plan an escape.

corporal, *n.* 1. Military rank. Used by the Independent Faction in the Unification War. Ranked below a lieutenant and a sergeant. *pr.n. uc.* 2. Title referring to rank held, e.g. Corporal Zoë Alleyne.

corral, *n.* 1. Fenced-in area built to contain livestock. In "Safe", the *Serenity* crew sets up a temporary corral to facilitate the sale of cattle. *v.* 2. Lead livestock into a corral with the intention of keeping them there.

Cortex, the, *pr.n.* The Alliance-owned complex communications, data-storage, and broadcasting network designed as the twenty-sixth-century equivalent of the internet. Its signal strength spans hundreds of planets and moons and is intensified

official

@ home w/ family (dinner)

front

Concilor

ABOVE: Shawna Trpcic's designs for the Councilor's costume.

BACK

by orbital satellites positioned around the Central planets. The Cortex is an integral part of society because of its ability to facilitate public and private messages called "waves", sharing of government or emergency-related alerts, data uploads and downloads, and customized searches. Ship pilots may access the Cortex via a console in the cockpit which is tied to the electrical system. Citizens in the technology-rich Central planets log into the Cortex on personal devices, public vidphones, Academy-owned consoles, etc. Elsewhere, Cortex access is limited to those who can afford the necessary equipment. This has led to a gap of information and data distribution, where the highest concentration of users is located in the Core. As such, the Alliance frequently uses the Cortex to share propaganda designed to benefit its interests and keep people in the Central planets in the dark.

cortical electrodes, *n. pl.* Medical device attached to the temples. Designed to stimulate brain activity in the cerebral cortex. Used in life-or-death situations.

Councilor, the, *pr.n.* Respected diplomat and member of the World Council governing the planet Ezra in the Georgia System. The Councilor holds a key political position that is also very demanding. She appeared in "War Stories" and, besides being Inara's client, supplied the dermal mender needed to reattach Mal's ear.

covered wagon, *n.* Type of horse-drawn vehicle built out of wood. The back, which usually holds personal belongings, supplies, or additional passengers, is covered with canvas to protect its contents from the elements and prying eyes. Settlers use covered wagons to travel on a Border planet or the rim. Seen at the beginning of "Our Mrs Reynolds".

crack, *n. sl.* Medical procedure to open the chest of a patient to access internal organs.

Crazy Ivan or **Ivan,** *pr.n.* Nickname for a risky ship maneuver Wash and Kaylee perform to escape Reavers in Whitefall's atmosphere during "Serenity".

ZOË: Full burn in atmo? That won't cause a blowback? Burn us out?

MAL: Even if it doesn't, they can push just as hard, keep right on us. Wash, you gotta give me an Ivan.

WASH: See what I can do ... (into com) Kaylee, how would you feel about pulling a Crazy Ivan?

KAYLEE: Always wanted to try one.
– "Serenity"

credits, *n. pl.* The official form of currency printed by the Anglo-Sino Alliance. Credits are reliably used in the Central planets because the system's primary economy relies on their use.

creed, *n.* Saying used to rally under dire circumstances. Also used as a golden rule to live by. "Leave no man behind" was the creed Wash told Jayne they needed to follow in "War Stories".

crime, *n.* Illegal activity punished in accordance with the law. Crime in the 'Verse is widespread and criminals are pursued and punished to varying degrees. The nature of crime ranges from high tech to low tech, from petty theft to the illegal manufacture of blastomeres. In general, two factors have a significant impact on how crooks and outlaws are prosecuted: location and social standing. A bank that was robbed on Jiangyin will be treated differently by law enforcement than a bank robbery on Persephone. Acts of vandalism committed by the son of an Alliance diplomat would be swept under the rug, while the salvage of a derelict ship without a permit by a Browncoat would result in an arrest. Most people throughout the known 'Verse have internalized how the Alliance upholds and enforces the law and use this information to either commit more crimes or band together with like-minded individuals. Matters related to interplanetary security and the Alliance are treated with the utmost importance. For those types of infractions, the Alliance devotes considerable time and resources to hunting down and capturing the fugitives who dared to question its authority.

crime syndicate, *n.* Illicit, well-organized group of people who commit crimes. Most crime syndicates are organized, led by a crime boss or small group of leaders, and have access to many resources. Crime syndicates tend to have a better footing than gangs or roving bands of thieves because their ill-gotten gains allow them to bribe the right people to look the other way. Adelai Niska, for example, is the head of a crime syndicate who bought off the World Council to ensure they looked the other way. While crime syndicates are often structured like a business, they aren't beholden to any ethical or moral responsibility which makes them as dangerous as any Alliance black ops program.

critters, *n. pl.* 1. Small animals. *n. pl. sl.* 2. Children or kids.

crop supplements, *n. pl.* Chemical additives, like fertilizer, applied to the soil to enhance the growth rate and yield of plants.

crop yield, *n.* Amount of fresh grains, vegetables, or fruit harvested from a field of produce. Yield varies based on the nutrients in the soil, the access to fresh water and sunlight, and the ability to remain in one place in order to maintain the fields. Unfortunately, the nutritional needs of a burgeoning population in a post-war environment are greater than the total yield currently produced, bought, and sold for the local communities. Thus, the lack of produce has driven up the price of fresh food. Travelers, city-dwellers, and spacefarers, like the *Serenity* crew, rarely have access to fresh produce unless they have the credits to pay for it. To make up for the lack of crops, protein bars are popularly consumed instead.

crops, *n. pl.* Fields of grain, fruit, or vegetables grown for human or animal consumption. Genetically-engineered seeds are given to new settlers to plant crops which, in theory, should provide a sustainable food source for their community. Commonly planted crops include: beans, corn, wheat, hay, and rye. These are planted throughout the 'Verse.

Crow, *pr.n.* Tattooed enforcer who worked for Adelai Niska. Spoke with a heavy accent. Part of a negotiation gone wrong in "The Train Job".

Crybaby, *n. sl.* A decoy that is jerry-rigged out of leftover parts and jettisoned out of a ship to put out a fake distress call and lead pursuers away. The decoy deployed by Wash in "Serenity" was Crybaby #6, and was contained within a Blue Sun Corporation coffee can.

MAL: Cry, baby, cry.

WASH (O.S.): Make your mother sigh. Engaging the Crybaby.

– "Serenity"

cryo, *adj.* 1. Related to the production of cold or extreme cold in organic or inorganic substances. *n. abbr.* 2. Short for cryonics or cryogenics. *adj.* 3. Of or pertaining to the field of cryonics or cryogenics. *n.* 4. In a cryonic or cryogenic state.

cryo lab, *n.* Scientific, sterile room where doctors and medical technicians apply the use of cryonics to their patients. St Lucy's Medical Hospital in Ariel City had a cryo lab.

cryo sleep, *n.* Induced state of rest caused by dropping the body temperature of a living patient down to extreme levels. In this condition, the patient is in stasis until revived at a later date.

cryo-box, *n.* Walled, insulated structure

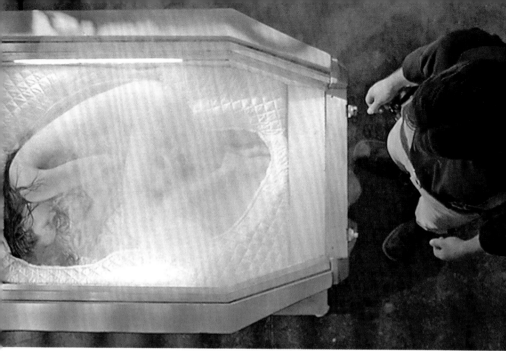

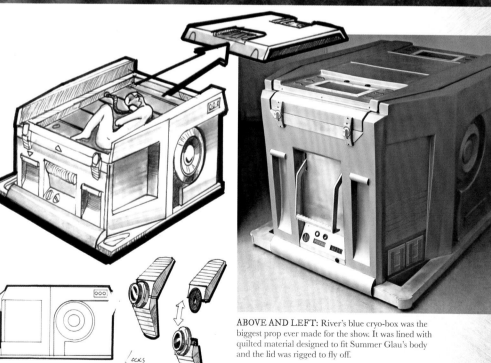

ABOVE AND LEFT: River's blue cryo-box was the biggest prop ever made for the show. It was lined with quilted material designed to fit Summer Glau's body and the lid was rigged to fly off.

designed to preserve the body of a single human in a cryonic state with the intention of reviving the patient at a later time. The equipment is high tech and use requires the help of a trained specialist and medical doctor.

cryogenics, *n.* Field of physics concerned with studying the effects of low to extremely low temperatures.

cryonics, *n.* Field of biology that deals with lowering the temperature of human tissue to preserve it for future use. Cryonics was initially developed to preserve the human body after death so it could be revived at a later date. In the twenty-sixth century, medical technology is so advanced that a living human body can be frozen to slow or halt the spread of disease while doctors and surgeons work on a cure for their patient.

currency, *n.* Money. An Alliance credit is the standard unit of currency accepted in the 'Verse. It is printed on paper and can be earned and exchanged digitally. Since credits are traceable, the criminally minded often prefer to make deals using platinum coins.

cuss, *adj.* 1. Pertaining to profanity. *v.* 2. The act of swearing. Cussing is considered sinful by Shepherds and a sign of ill-manners by most members of high society in the Core. The type and frequency of curse words used in a person's vocabulary may also indicate where they hail from in the 'Verse.

cyanosis, *n.* Skin with a bluish or purple tint caused by low oxygen levels in the blood.

cyanotic, *adj.* Pertaining to a blue skin discoloration.

ABOVE: These Alliance credits, created for the show, were inspired by Thai banknotes and printed on parchment, which was then cut by hand.

D.C. line, *n.* Name of a feed used in ships. Referred to in "Bushwhacked".

Dalin, *pr.n.* Niska's new henchman in "War Stories". He replaced Crow.

Damp Lung or **Damplung,** *n. sl.* Respiratory illness where fluid accumulates in the lungs. Similar to pneumonia.

dandy, *n. masc.* Man obsessed with his physical appearance, the clothes he wears, and the company he keeps.

darkness, the, *n. sl.* 1. Negative connotation of space. Synonym for "the black". *n. sl.* 2. Pure evil.

datastick, *n.* Thin, pen-shaped rod containing audio-visual data related to a body of knowledge. Simon Tam has collected the following datasticks: Medical Science, Universal Encyclopedia, Anatomical Engineering, Bio-Physical Areas, Human History, and Languages.

day, *n.* Unit of time. Most terraformed planets were selected to closely resemble Earth-That-Was, so the length of a day is typically similar with some variations.

Deadwood, *pr.n.* Planet in the Blue Sun System. The Heart of Gold is located here.

derelict, *adj.* 1. Broken. In bad shape. Neglected. *n.* 2. Ship floating aimlessly through space. *n.* 3. Homeless vagrant.

dermal mender, *n.* High-tech medical equipment designed to refasten two pieces of flesh together. At the conclusion of "War Stories", Simon used a dermal mender to reattach Mal's ear.

desperados, *n. pl.* Bold, daring, reckless lawbreakers. Dauntless criminals who act rashly, not caring if they'll be caught.

Destra, *pr.n.* Socialite and friend of Banning Miller in "Shindig".

Device, The, *pr.n.* Cutting-edge weapon in the shape of a rod with a blue light. The Device emits a high-pitched sonic wave that targets a victim's brain. An attack from this weapon is fatal. Blue-gloved agents, described by River Tam as the "hands of blue", used The Device in "Ariel".

devil, *n.* 1. The personification of evil. Belief in the devil is still alive and well in 2517, and is stronger in isolated settlements. *adj.* 2. Synonym for evil: people or objects.

"Damn you, Bridget! Damn you ta Hades! You broke my heart in a million pieces! You made me love you, and then y – I SHAVED MY BEARD FOR YOU, DEVIL WOMAN!"

– Monty, "Trash"

devil woman, *n. fem. sl.* Evil woman. Insult thrown at a woman who's left a trail of broken hearts in her wake.

diagnostic, *adj.* 1. Of or pertaining to the medical diagnosis of a patient's health. *n.* 2. Physical scans, images, or other important data that's related to a doctor's diagnosis for a patient, e.g. "River's brain scan is a diagnostic."

diagnostic ward, *n.* Twenty-sixth-century equivalent of a hospital X-ray room. The diagnostic ward is high tech and uses 3D technology to capture a detailed image of a human body part, like the brain or a bone, for examination.

digital paper, *n.* Thin carbon sheet that displays, records, and stores information, replacing the need for paper and writing utensils like a pen or pencil. Digital paper is more commonly found on the Central planets than on the Border planets or the rim. Badger uses a piece of digital paper in his office during "Serenity".

dilate, *v.* Become wider, more open, e.g. "This medicine will dilate your pupils."

dilavtin, *n.* Standarized medicine admin-istered to patients to prep them for surgery. Simon refers to dilavtin in "Ariel".

dining area, *n.* Common room on a ship where the crew eats and spends time together. In the military, commonly referred to as a mess hall.

distress signal, *n.* Beacon emitted to relay a ship's emergency status.

divorce, *n.* Legal separation of spouses. Rules governing divorce vary widely across the 'Verse and the ability to end a marriage often depends on religious/cultural beliefs.

DNA test device, *n.* Portable, self-contained device designed to extract DNA from an expectant mother in order to determine the identity of the father. Rance Burgess used this device to confirm Petaline's child was his in "Heart of Gold".

Dobson, Lawrence, *pr.n.* Friendly-faced federal marshall and Alliance mole who tracked Simon Tam to *Serenity* in order to recapture his sister, River. Dobson relied on a variety of psychological tactics in addition to his use of raw, physical force to help him infiltrate and manipulate the crew. He appeared in "Serenity".

OPPOSITE: The *Serenity* dining area, attached to the galley.

RIGHT: A DNA test device, as seen in "Heart of Gold", was used by Rance Burgess to threaten Petaline (see above).

FAR RIGHT: The Device, a protoype weapon, used by the mysterious hands of blue in "Ariel".

DOBSON: Let me speak a language you will understand. Money. This girl is worth a lot of money. I mean a lot. You kill me, there's nothing. But you help me out, you'll have enough to buy your own ship. A better one than this piece of crap.

JAYNE: Does helping you out mean turning on the Captain?

DOBSON: Yes it does.

JAYNE: (Pauses) Let's talk money, Larry.

– "Serenity"

dock, *v.* 1. Act of a ship being attached to a ship, ramp, airlock, or platform in space or on land. Docking allows passengers and cargo to be transported safely from one point to another. *n.* 2. Physical location where a ship is stored. Also referred to as a spacedock. Examples include Eavesdown Docks on Persephone and the off-screen spacedock in Li Shen's Space Bazaar.

Doralee, *pr.n.* Superstitious schoolteacher/ nurse who lives in an isolated town on Jiangyin. While well-meaning, she is uneducated and easily spooked by the unknown. Doralee accused River Tam of witchcraft in "Safe".

down to the wire, *id.* Tense situation caused by running out of time or a specific substance, like fuel or bullets. The outcome is anybody's guess.

drawers, *n. pl. sl.* Underwear. Boxers or longjohns, e.g. "Before the shootin' starts, at least let me pull up my drawers."

drive feed, *n.* Wires on a ship that transmit power to the cockpit. Part of the navigational system.

drone, *n.* Automated mechanical object programmed to fire bullets or record audio-visual data. Used primarily for military purposes and typically unavailable for personal or commercial use.

duel, *n.* Arranged fight between two individuals governed by a set of specific

LEFT: Malcolm Reynolds and Atherton Wing duel at Cadrie Pond on Persephone. Mal unwittingly challenged Atherton when he punched him during a dance in "Shindig". Lord Warwick Harrow then volunteered to be Mal's second.

rules. Punching/slapping someone's face will trigger a duel if these rules are observed. The location, weapons, time to prepare, funerary arrangements, substitute fighters, and winning conditions are governed by these rules. In "Shindig", Mal punched his opponent, Atherton Wing, in the face. Atherton claimed this had triggered a duel and, as the challenged party, chose swords as the weapon of choice. Lord Warrick Harrow was Mal's second, and the duel took place at Cadrie Pond. Typically, a duel is considered a "gentleman's fight" and is part of high societal culture.

GENTLEMAN: There has been a challenge!

ATHERTON WING: I hope you're prepared, Captain.

MAL: You all talkin' 'bout a fight? Well, fine, let's get out of here!

INARA: It's not a fist fight, Mal.

GENTLEMAN: The duel will be met tomorrow morning, at Cadrie Pond.

MAL: Why wait? Where's that guard? He collected a whole mess a' pistols—

GENTLEMAN: If you require it, any gentleman here can give you use of a sword.

MAL: Use of a ... s'what?

– "Shindig"

dulcimer, *n.* Type of musical instrument. There are two models. The first is a trapezoidal-shaped box that has a series of tightened strings attached to both sides. Each string represents a unique musical note. To play music, a musician uses a pair of hammers to strike the strings. The second is a string instrument with a round body and a fret board. It may be played using the fingers or a bow.

dumper, *n. sl.* Ship that's a piece of trash. A junker. Often used as an insult to describe older models, like a Firefly-class boat.

dumpling, *n.* 1. Food made from dough. Can be plain or stuffed. *n. sl.* 2. Term of endearment, e.g. "You're my lil' dumpling."

dunghead, *n. sl.* Less vulgar way of saying "shithead", but means the same thing. Name to call a jerk or an asshole.

dungheap, *n. sl.* Pile of shit. Name used to describe a location that's in terrible condition. Synonym for shithole.

Durban, Rance, *pr.n.* Victim murdered on Jiangyin by the Grange brothers.

Duul, Ammon, *pr.n.* Alliance Postmaster General in charge of the Allied Postal Service outpost located on Li Shen's Space Bazaar. Duul is threatened by Lieutenant Womack in "Safe".

dyna-ram, *n.* Electrical part of an automated trash bin. In "Trash", when Jayne attempted to switch out the controls, he accidentally touched this piece and was knocked out from being electrocuted.

Dyton Colony, *pr.n.* Government-sanctioned settlement located on a moon that orbits the planet Greenleaf in the Red Sun System. Dyton is considered part of the Border planets.

E.C.G. or **E.K.G.**, *n. abbr.* Electro- cardiogram. Common test that scans the electrical activity in the heart to identify and diagnose health problems.

E.M.T., *n. abbr.* Emergency Medical Technician. A responder trained to help stabilize patients in life-or-death situations and then transport them to a nearby hospital. Identified by a badge that grants hospital access. E.M.T.s wear uniforms that bear a patch denoting their position.

E.R., *n. abbr.* Hospital emergency room.

Early, Jubal, *pr.n.* Bountyhunter in pursuit of River during "Objects in Space".

Earth-That-Was, *pr.n.* Name given to Earth after it was abandoned and destroyed. In the twenty-sixth century, all people refer to Earth as Earth-That-Was.

Earth-That-Was memorabilia, *pr.n.* Artifacts that have survived the passage of time after humanity left Earth. These relics are over 500 years old and are considered extremely valuable if not priceless. While the condition of such memorabilia ranges broadly, most collectors proudly seek it out and display it regardless as a sign of their wealth and status. Adelai Niska and

RIGHT: Mal and Jayne pose as E.M.T.s in "Ariel". Their uniforms are authentic to avoid suspicion.

ABOVE: Durran Haymer is a known collector of Earth-That-Was memorabilia and prized artifacts, like the Lassiter.

SAFFRON: Do you know the myth of Earth-That-Was?

WASH: Not so much.

SAFFRON: That when she was born, she had no sky, and she was open, inviting, and the stars would rush into her, through the skin of her, making the oceans boil with sensation, and when she could endure no more ecstasy, she puffed up her cheeks and blew out the sky, to womb her and keep them at bay, 'til she had rest some, and that we had to leave 'cause she was strong enough to suck them in once more.

– From *"Our Mrs Reynolds"*

Little by little, the tribes used the Earth up. Barren, she had little left to offer them. Swollen of her, they left. And for the first time since the Great Burn that birthed her, she was alone.
The Earth cried, and terrible were her tears. Acid and caustic, the spawn of the tribes' rape. They flowed a century.
The fire that finally came did so as a blessing.

–English translation from play in "Heart of Gold"

Durran Haymer are examples of two individuals who own Earth-That-Was memorabilia.

Earth-That-Was myths, *pr.n. pl.* Even though humanity left Earth-that-Was for a clear reason, this event happened approximately 500 years ago. With each passing generation, the stories about Earth-That-Was have evolved, reflecting the diversity of cultures found in the 'Verse. Some myths are religious or philosophical. Others are embedded with a moral lesson or teaching. Though the details, formats, and performances of these stories may change depending on the storyteller(s), Earth-That-Was myths are the one thread that ties humanity, in all of its diversity, together.

Eavesdown Docks, *pr.n.* City located on Persephone at the edge of the White Sun System. Eavesdown Docks has a lot to offer travelers, smugglers, socialites, and residents. The city boasts futuristic skyscrapers as well as a spacedock where crews entice passengers to come aboard. It also has a municipal transit system, several shops and services, and a criminal underground. Badger lives in Eavesdown Docks, and the city is a frequent destination for the *Serenity* crew.

eighty-oh-four, *n. abbr.* Abbreviated description of a ship model. Kaylee referred to this when she was holding court in "Shindig" during the dance.

Eighty-Second, *pr.n. abbr.* The unit that

BELOW: Production designs for Eavesdown Docks on Persephone, the home of Badger and a frequent jump-off point for the crew of *Serenity*.

Credit: Charles Ratteray

was ordered to stand down and abandon the Independents in the Battle of Serenity.

eighty-ten, *n. abbr.* An eighty-oh-four model that has fancier hull plating so that it might look like a different ship.

electromagnetic net or **net,** *n.* Illegal mechanical device used to steal and trap ships. The net's frame is a giant metal ring that's large enough to contain a ship. A series of small electromagnetic transmitters are embedded into intervals on the interior of the net. By itself, the frame is not dangerous to ships or humans unless it is turned on. When activated, the transmitters emit a charge forming lines of electromagnetic energy that recreate the appearance and function of a fisherman's net. Ships that come into contact with the center of the ring are then trapped. The energy from the net turns the ship into a conductor and electrocutes anyone who's still inside the ship. The nets are ineffective

if a single transmitter is damaged. Jayne Cobb shot a transmitter to set *Serenity* free in "Our Mrs Reynolds".

'em, *n. abbr.* Short for the pronoun "them". While it's not a slang word, the use of 'em indicates the speaker may live outside the Central planets. It is considered improper to not say the full word, e.g. "Let's get 'em!"

emergency signal ring, *n.* Personal safety device that, when activated, sends a beacon to local law officials. Worn by high-ranking members of Alliance society. Durran Haymer wore and activated this ring in "Safe" on Bellerophon.

engine room, *n.* Area of the ship containing tools, equipment, and systems required to maintain and operate the ship's movements. The engines are a crucial part of a ship that require oversight by a mechanic or specialist. The larger the ship, the larger the engine, and the more maintenance is required.

ensign, *n.* Lowest rank for an Alliance soldier assigned to an Alliance cruiser.

Escobar, *pr.n.* Military police officer under Commander Harken in "Bushwhacked". He and Keene are ordered to prevent the Survivor (or proto-Reaver) from getting back on the Alliance cruiser.

extenders, *n. pl.* Mechanical parts that stabilize an engine to prevent the ship from shaking and rattling as it rotates.

extractor, *n.* Surgical instrument designed to remove a bullet. Simon Tam asks for this in "Serenity".

Ezra, *pr.n.* Border planet with a desert landscape in the Georgia System. Niska's Skyplex orbits this planet. Below the Skyplex, independent operators like Bolles traffic goods on the black market.

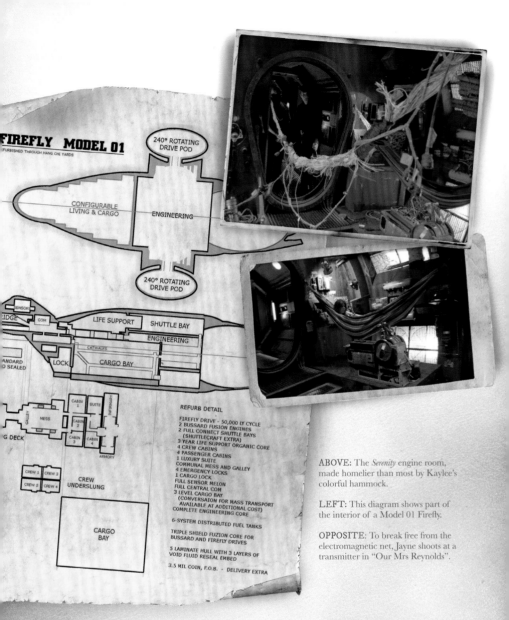

FIREFLY MODEL 01
FURBISHED THROUGH HANG CHI YARDS

240° ROTATING DRIVE POD

CONFIGURABLE LIVING & CARGO

ENGINEERING

240° ROTATING DRIVE POD

SENSOR

BRIDGE   COM

LIFE SUPPORT   SHUTTLE BAY

ENGINEERING

CATWALKS

STANDARD TO SEALED

LOCK   CARGO BAY

GALLEY   CABIN 1   SUITE   INFIRMARY

MESS   CABIN 2

G DECK   CABIN 3   CABIN 4

ARMORY

CREW 1   CREW 3
CREW 2   CREW 4

CREW UNDERSLUNG

CARGO BAY

REFURB DETAIL

FIREFLY DRIVE – 50,000 LY CYCLE
2 BUSSARD FUSION ENGINES
2 FULL CONNECT SHUTTLE BAYS
   (SHUTTLECRAFT EXTRA)
3 YEAR LIFE SUPPORT ORGANIC CORE
4 CREW CABINS
4 PASSENGER CABINS
1 LUXURY SUITE
COMMUNAL MESS AND GALLEY
4 EMERGENCY LOCKS
1 CARGO LOCK
FULL SENSOR MELON
FULL CENTRAL COM
3 LEVEL CARGO BAY
   (CONVERSATION FOR MASS TRANSPORT
   AVAILABLE AT ADDITIONAL COST)
COMPLETE ENGINEERING CORE

6-SYSTEM DISTRIBUTED FUEL TANKS

TRIPLE SHIELD FUZION CORE FOR
BUSSARD AND FIREFLY DRIVES

5 LAMINATE HULL WITH 3 LAYERS OF
VOID FLUID RESEAL EMBED

3.5 MIL COIN, F.O.B. · DELIVERY EXTRA

ABOVE: The *Serenity* engine room, made homelier than most by Kaylee's colorful hammock.

LEFT: This diagram shows part of the interior of a Model 01 Firefly.

OPPOSITE: To break free from the electromagnetic net, Jayne shoots at a transmitter in "Our Mrs Reynolds".

That pattern you're looking at is a net. We fly into that we're more than helpless. It'll turn the ship into one big electrical conduit, burns us all from the inside out." – Malcolm Reynolds, "Our Mrs Reynolds"

faith, *n.* 1. Individual belief in a higher power. Driving force behind a person's actions, especially in times of duress or danger. *n.* 2. Religion. The 'Verse incorporates many different faiths with the two most dominant being Buddhism and Christianity. The parent religions incorporate many branches of faiths that have sprung up in isolated communities, around religious leaders or prophets, or in contention with the primary religion's interpretation of religious texts and practices. Though these branches are still considered part of the parent religion, their customs and beliefs are typically different. The Triumph Settlers are an example of believers who branched away from Christianity to form their own customs.

Their beliefs greatly differ from the primary faith practiced by Shepherds, and incorporate many traditions. Buddhism, which is practiced by Companions and many people within the Core, was not as dominant in the places the *Serenity* crew visited during the show. However it, too, shares branches that have occurred as a result of humanity spreading out across multiple planetary systems.

fancible, *adj. sl.* Of frilly or being all dressed up. Colloquial use of the word "fancy".

fare, *n.* Payment given to the owner and operator of a ship, train, bus, or other public or private form of transportation in exchange for safe passage to a new destination. Fares are typically paid for using local currency or valuable items

ABOVE: Shepherd Book's faith shapes his personality, appearance, and language. His hair is kept according to the rules of his order. He also carries a Bible with him wherever he goes.

by way of trade, like Shepherd Book's produce and spices in "Serenity".

fast burn rocket shuttle, *n.* Small, short-range shuttle that leaves a telltale black mark when it flies. Typically attached to a space station, like Niska's Skyplex. Referred to in "War Stories".

fed, *n. abbr.* Generic term for a federal agent or marshall. A federal marshall has a larger jurisdiction than local law enforcement, and the right to pursue fugitives and suspects.

fed station, *n. abbr.* Federal station. Official building where agents work and share information. Fed stations are located throughout the 'Verse and, outside of the Core, are often found near a colony or Alliance outpost filled with soldiers.

Fendris, *pr.n.* Lieutenant Womack's backup. An officer of the law who'd been corrupted by whatever Womack promised him. Appears in "The Message".

fib, *v.* To lie or deceive.

fiddle, *v.* 1. Tinker with a mechanical console or part to restore/alter functionality. *n.* 2. String instrument belonging to the violin family.

57th Overlanders, *pr.n.* Independent Faction military unit that fought in the Unification War. Present at the Battle of Du-Khang and the Battle of Serenity. Members included Sergeant Malcolm Reynolds, Corporal Zoë Alleyne, and Private Tracey Smith.

filament, *n.* Ultra-thin wire or thread-like fiber, like a strand of hair.

firefight, *n.* 1. Military term describing a battle where gunfire was exchanged between two sides. *n. sl.* 2. Since the Unification War, some veterans and mercenaries have adopted the term in a negative context to relay the severity of a bloody gunfight.

Firefly, *pr.n.* Class of ship. Mal's ship, *Serenity*, is a Firefly. According to Commander Harken in "Bushwhacked", there are approximately 50,000 Firefly-class ships flying outside the Core.

first mate, *n.* Second-in-command of a

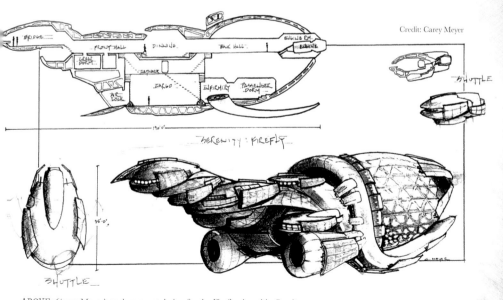

Credit: Carey Meyer

ABOVE: Carey Meyer's early concept design for the Firefly-class ship *Serenity*.

ABOVE: Zoic's CG model of *Serenity* based on earlier sketches.

"Midbulk transport, standard radion-accelerator core, classcode 03-K64, 'Firefly'." – River, "The Train Job"

private vessel. Zoë Alleyne Washburne is Captain Reynolds' first mate.

flap your gums, *id.* Speak idly and without purpose. A negative observation of a person who shouldn't have spoken or revealed information, e.g. "You think flapping your gums is going to help our situation?"

flash, *n.* 1. Impressive, ostentatious style. Outrageously expensive. *n.* 2. Bright burst of light. *v.* 3. Briefly show then remove. *n. sl.* 4. Shortest period of time. A second or a moment that went by too quickly.

flash grenade or **stun grenade,** *n.* Type of weapon thrown to temporarily blind enemy targets and dull their senses.

flash my ass, *id.* Drawing attention to oneself by intentionally provoking the viewer.

flesh, *n. sl.* 1. Bare (naked) skin. *n.* 2. Human tissue.

float, *v.* Drift aimlessly in space.

florid, *adj.* Intricate and excessively ornate. Unnecessarily elaborate.

folk, *n.* People. Commonly used on the Border planets and the rim. May be accompanied by a gender-specific term like menfolk, girlfolk, etc.

foodstuffs, *n. pl.* Synthetic or natural substances that are considered to be food.

foofaraw, *n. sl.* 1. Unnecessary frills or lace. *n. sl.* 2. Great deal of attention spent on a minor subject or event. A fuss made over nothing.

KAYLEE: (pointing) Say. Look at the fluffy one.

ZOË: Too much foofaraw. If I'm gonna wear a
dress, I want something with slink.

– "Shindig"

ABOVE: Example of a force field used in place
of glass or plastic windows. Seen in "The Train Job".

force field, *n.* Barrier made out of energy
particles that, when activated, creates
a physical plane. Twenty-sixth-century
invention used for a variety of private,
commercial, and military purposes. One
of the most commonly found force fields is
the one created to replace glass windows in
buildings. At the beginning of "The Train
Job", a tavern's force field was deactivated
and Mal was thrown out of the hole.

fore, *adj.* Toward or at the nose of a ship, e.g.
"The foredeck directly leads to the bridge."

fore-couple, *n.* Ship part that links two
other pieces of equipment together.
Positioned toward the front of the ship, as
opposed to the reg-couple, which is located
toward the rear.

foreman, *n.* High-ranking manager. A
foreman oversees the business at Canton
Mudworks, and gives commands to the

prods, who manage the workers.

formal charge, *n.* Literal description of
a crime attributed to a lawbreaker that is
shared with officials in order to record the
crime and decide the suspect's fate. Formal
charges match the legal definitions of
crimes as defined by the Alliance.

freighter, *n.* Bulkier type of ship usually
used to transport goods or people.

Friedlich's, *pr.n.* Fine restaurant located in
Capital City on Osiris in the Central planets.

frippery, *n.* Ostentatious, gaudy embellish-
ments on a piece of clothing.

BELOW: Tim Earls' design for Monty's
freighter, as seen in "Trash".

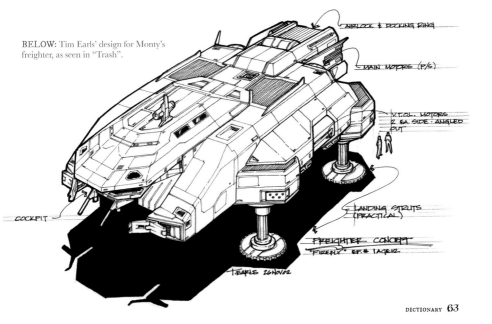

Kaywinnet Lee "Kaylee" Frye

Cheerful and bubbly to a fault, *Serenity*'s ship mechanic is comfortable speaking in technobabble, using words like "synchronizers", "extenders" and "plating" with ease. When she's talking about ships, Kaylee communicates well with Wash, but has to translate what she's saying to characters like Mal who don't have the same aptitude for mechanical engineering as she does.

Kaylee's dialogue is casual regardless of where she is or who she's with, which speaks to her upbringing on a Border planet. To reflect her background, Kaylee will drop the "g" from words ending in -ing like "tellin'", and will also speak colloquially instead of formally. While she doesn't shorten her sentences as much as Jayne does, the mechanic will often preface her lines with filler words like "So", "Oh", "Look", and "Well". She'll also abbreviate certain words such as "'cause".

Though her favorite word is "shiny", Kaylee has been known to curse on occasion in Chinese and English. Typically, however, Kaylee doesn't resort to vulgar usages and her preferred curse words are less offensive than Mal's or Jayne's.

"Don't you just love this party? Everything's so fancy, and there's some kind of hot cheese over there. " – "Shindig"

Kaylee-speak:

"This girl knows her ships."

"Simon! Whole point of swearin' is that it ain't appropriate."

"No power in the 'Verse can stop me!"

frontal lobe, *n.* Area of the brain responsible for the ability to control emotions and other key components of a personality including memory, judgment, problem-solving, and language.

Frye, Kaywinnet Lee "Kaylee", *pr.n.* Intuitive ship mechanic with no formal training who has a cheerful and positive attitude. In "Out of Gas", it's revealed that she joined the *Serenity* crew after proving her knowledge and fixing the ship. She is considered to be the heart of the ship and is well-loved by the crew.

fuel cell, *n.* Unit of semi-solid material engineered to be a safe power supply for spaceships.

fuel reserve, *n.* Backup power supply used by ships in emergency situations.

fugitive, *n.* Outlaw who has been formally charged, but is now on the run from law enforcement. Simon and River Tam are considered fugitives.

full burn, *v.* Act of maximizing the use of a ship's engines. Burns all fuel.

full-yield, *adj.* Of the maximum amount that can be returned. Generally used when describing bombs or munitions. A full-yield mag drop, for example, has ensured the maximum amount of damage.

funerary customs, *n. pl.* Prayers and ceremonies to put the dead to rest. Saying a prayer for the dead is part of Shepherd Book's responsibilities as a preacher, and he believes that this is a necessary task even when traveling in the black. Customs, however, aren't standardized and vary as widely as marriage rites do. Depending upon the beliefs of the deceased and loved ones, the ceremony may incorporate other cultural customs as a show of respect, as was the case with Nandi's Buddhist-Christian burial. Funerals took place in "Bushwhacked", "The Message", and "Heart of Gold".

funny, *adj.* 1. Humorous, as in laughing after a joke. *adj.* 2. Odd or unusual. *adj.* 3. Of a person or object that appears suspicious.

BELOW: Tracey Smith's body is laid to rest in snowy St Albans. Greg Edmonson recalls composing the mournful funeral music in this scene more as a tribute to the show than for Tracey himself.

ABOVE: The *Serenity* galley was fitted with aircraft lockers to keep the crew's food in situ on bumpy journeys.

galley, *n.* Kitchen located on a ship.

gallows, *n. pl.* Constructed frame built to kill a victim by hanging. Commonly found on the Border planets and rim. It is a cheap form of executing criminals; the death is often conducted in public.

geisha doll, *n.* Effigy of a Japanese courtesan manufactured as a toy or collectible.

Gen-seed, *pr.n.* Genetically engineered seed given to settlers to grow hardy, bug-resistant crops in a variety of soils. The Alliance includes Gen-seed in every crate of supplies destined for a Border world or the rim. Valued by smugglers and criminals due to its high selling price on the black market.

Georgia System, *pr.n.* Planetary system that forms part of the Border planets encompassing the Core. Regina, Whitefall, and Ezra are examples of its celestial bodies.

g-line, *n.* Name of a wire that is found in the cockpit. Part of the ship.

going dark, *id.* Act of turning off the majority of the ship's power to avoid detection by another ship.

Gommen, Elder, *pr.n.* Leader of the

Triumph Settlement. After *Serenity*'s crew took out the bandits plaguing the community, Elder Gommen rewarded them with a party. Mal got a wife and Jayne received a rainstick. In an unaired scene, it is revealed that Elder Gommen knew Saffron and was in on the con.

goodnight kiss, *n. sl.* Act of kissing and knocking a victim unconscious. A woman wears lipstick laced with fast-acting narcotics that, upon contact with her target's lips, are immediately absorbed into the bloodstream. This puts the victim in a medically-induced sleep for several hours before they wake up with a nasty headache.

MAL: How did ...

SIMON: A narcotic compound, probably spread over a seal on her lips. You get it on yours and pow.

ZOË: Lips, huh?

MAL: Well, no ...

SIMON: We used to get a lot of guys brought in on the night shift at the E.R. – usually robbed and very groggy. Called it the 'goodnight kiss'.

– "Our Mrs Reynolds"

gorramn or **gorram,** *interj. vul.* A swear word unique to the 'Verse, that allows the crew to curse without taking the Lord's name in vain. Equivalent of goddamn.

gorramnitall, *interj. vul.* Gorramn it all! Used when a person's luck goes south in a hurry. Cursing the world. Equivalent of goddamnitall.

government stamp, *n.* Official seal of the Anglo-Sino Alliance. Used to mark crates of supplies and specific goods like protein bars.

Grange brothers, *pr.n. pl.* Marcus and Nathaniel Grange made a deal with Badger to buy cattle from Captain Reynolds. They

ABOVE: The chopsticks used in the galley are a mix of various different cultures – from the basic wooden sticks found on the rim to expensive Core planet lacquerware.

are arrested for the murder of Rance Durban and killed in a shoot-out during "Safe".

gravboot, *n.* Cover that's attached to a part of the gravity drive on a ship.

grav-dampener, *n.* Ship part that's integral to the gravity drive.

graveyard, *n.* 1. Place where dead bodies are buried. *n. sl.* 2. Shipwreck or area of space where derelict ships can be found.

gravity drive, *n.* Ship system responsible for creating and maintaining artificial gravity while flying through space.

Graydon, *pr.n.* An Independent radio operator who fought alongside Sergeant Malcolm Reynolds during the Battle of Serenity. Graydon was promoted to the rank of lieutenant following the death of Lieutenant Baker. He died shortly afterward.

Greenleaf, *pr.n.* Planet in the Red Sun System. One of the Border planets.

Grizwald, *pr.n.* Uniquely designed grenade that's hidden inside an apple, then thrown to enemy lines.

ZOË: Do you know what a Grizwald is?

JAYNE: It's a grenade.

ZOË: 'Bout the size of a battery. Responds to pressure. Our platoon was stuck in a trench outside New Kasmir during the winter campaign ... More'n'a week, completely cut off, and the Alliance entrenched not ten yards away. We even got to talking with 'em, yelling across insults and jokes and such, 'cause no ammo to speak of, no orders, what are you gonna do? We mentioned we were out of rations and ten minutes later a bunch'a apples rained into the trench.

– "War Stories"

groggy, *adj.* Of a physical state of being that happens as a result of regaining consciousness after taking a drug, or the hazy state that follows waking up. Sleepy. Tired. Out of it.

ABOVE: Zoë pushes a gurney through St Lucy's Medical Center in "Ariel".

Gruviek, *pr.n.* Former middleman Captain Reynolds once worked with. Killed by Reavers. Referenced in "Serenity".

guffaw, *n. sl.* Loud fuss over nothing. Unnecessary argument.

Guild, *pr.n.* An Alliance-sanctioned, legal organization made up of smaller, specialized groups called "guilds".

Guild Law, *pr.n.* Rules governing the legal rights of Alliance citizens. Details matters pertaining to Companions, trade, salvage, commerce, crime, etc. In most cases, a permit or ident card is required to perform most basic functions. This allows the Alliance to keep tabs on its citizens, especially since they are spread across many planets and moons.

gun scan, *n.* Electronic screening to prevent an individual from bringing a weapon into an event.

gunplay, *n. sl.* Fight where pistols are fired. Typically used when no one involved was shot, injured, or killed.

gurney, *n.* Mobile stretcher with wheels used to transport patients and corpses into a medical facility, like a hospital.

Gurtlser engine, *pr.n.* Type of engine that shakes a ship when she flies. Kaylee told Book the *Paragon* was equipped with one.

H

haggle, *v.* To negotiate the terms of a deal for a better outcome. Guild-sanctioned traders and smugglers both like to haggle and come to new terms. Barter is common outside the Core, where the finer things in life are in short supply.

hair, *n.* Integral part of culture throughout the known 'Verse. May be grown long, kept in a certain style, shaved off, etc.

halloo, *interj.* Greeting. Synonym for hello.

Hancock, *pr.n.* 1. City located on the planet Regina in the Georgia System. Referenced in "Safe". *n. sl.* 2. A signature.

hands of blue, *id.* Mysterious agents in pursuit of River Tam who wear suits and blue gloves. Their authority and clearance, despite the fact that they are contractors, is higher than an agent or Alliance commander. Their first appearance was at the end of "The Train Job". When they appeared in "Ariel", they wielded a high-tech sonic device that murdered the Alliance officers on duty at St Lucy's Medical Center.

Harbatkin, Captain, *pr.n.* Alias Mal used

when he docked with the *I.A.V. Magellan* in "Safe" to get Shepherd Book medical help.

Harken, Commander, *pr.n.* Leader of an Alliance cruiser who accused the *Serenity* crew of killing and mutilating settlers in "Bushwhacked". He did not believe that Reavers were real, until it was too late. Captain Reynolds saved his life.

Harrow, Sir Warrick, *pr.n.* Owner of an unbranded herd of cattle who decided to hire the *Serenity* crew to transport the goods and conduct an illicit sale. He holds a title of "lord" and is a member of the nobility. Appeared in "Shindig".

Haymer, Durran, *pr.n.* Former bio-weapons expert and insanely rich owner of a private estate on Bellerophon. Owns a considerable collection of Earth-That-Was artifacts and historical objects, like the Lassiter. Husband to Yolanda, and the target of the robbery in "Trash".

Head of Surgery, *pr.n.* Leadership position held by a medical doctor in a hospital. It is a prestigious and high-paying role.

Heart of Gold, *pr.n.* Name of a brothel

BELOW: The enigmatic "hands of blue" are on the hunt for River Tam in "Ariel".

Hero of Canton

Jayne! The Man they call Jayne!

He robbed from the rich and he gave to the poor
He stood up to the Man and he gave him what for
Our love for him now ain't hard to explain
The Hero of Canton, the man they call Jayne!

Our Jayne saw the Mudders' backs breakin'
He saw the Mudders lament
And he saw that magistrate takin'
Every dollar and leavin' five cents
So he said, "You can't do that to my people.
You can't crush them under your heel"
Jayne strapped on his hat
And in five seconds flat
Stole everything Boss Higgins had to steal

He robbed from the rich and he gave to the poor
Stood up to the Man and he gave him what for
Our love for him now ain't hard to explain
The Hero of Canton, the man they call Jayne!

Now here is what separates heroes
From common folk like you and I
The man they call Jayne
He turned round his plane
And let that money hit sky

He dropped it onto our houses
He dropped it into our yards
And the man they call Jayne
He turned round his plane
And headed out for the stars

He robbed from the rich and he gave to the poor
Stood up to the Man and he gave him what for
Our love for him now ain't hard to explain
The Hero of Canton, the man they call Jayne!

BELOW: Jayne, the Hero of Canton, stands before his statue on the mud-farming moon. Show writer Ben Edlund was inspired for this setting when he read about the development of high-tech ceramics and became interested in "the notion of fusing high-tech sci-fi with a really low-tech town of lumpen proletariat masses".

ABOVE: Stitch Hessian, Jayne's former partner in crime, comes back unexpectedly to kill Canton's beloved hero and get his revenge for Jayne's betrayal.

on the planet Deadwood that was run by Nandi, an unlicensed Companion. After her death, Petaline took over.

heat scan, *n.* Type of probe that targets an area or ship, searching for signs of life by examining heat signatures.

Heinrich, *pr.n.* Young security programmer Yolanda Haymer murdered to earn her freedom. She stole his ship. Referenced in "Trash".

Helen, *pr.n.* Prostitute who works in the "Heart of Gold".

helm, *n.* Ship controls. To "take the helm" is to sit in front of the controls and navigate the ship, relieving another person of their duty.

hence, *adv.* 1. Indicates a future point in time when added after a temporal measurement, e.g. "Four years hence" or "Two months hence". *adv.* 2. Used in causal relationships when reaching a conclusion, e.g. "Hence, I think we should go to Ariel."

Hero of Canton, *pr.n.* 1. Jayne Cobb. *pr.n.* 2. Title of a song written in Jayne's honor.

Hessian, Stitch, *pr.n.* Jayne Cobb's former partner who was captured after attempting to rob Magistrate Higgins. Jayne pushed him off the ship to lessen its weight and therefore get free and clear. Stitch was imprisoned in a hotbox and released to kill Jayne in "Jaynestown". Now deceased.

Higgins, Fess, *pr.n.* Son of Magistrate Higgins and heir to the Canton Mudworks empire. He became Inara's client at the urging of his father in order to lose his virginity. Later, he defied his father and set

the crew free after he cancelled a land-lock. Appeared in "Jaynestown".

Higgins, Magistrate, *pr.n.* Ruthless Alliance ruler, owner of Canton Mudworks, and sanctioned owner of Higgins' Moon. Has a large estate and flaunts his wealth, which he does not share with the indentured workers who harvest the mud for his factory.

Higgins' Moon, *pr.n.* Moon owned and operated by Magistrate Higgins in the Red Sun System. Orbits the planet Harvest.

hisself, *pr.* Colloquial pronunciation of "himself".

hitched, *v. sl.* Married.

hodgeberry, *n.* Edible fruit that grows on a bush. Simon and River ate hodgeberries in "Safe", which triggered a flashback of when they were growing up on Osiris.

Holden boys, *pr.n. pl.* Middlemen Captain Reynolds has worked with in the past. While they are criminals, they avoid running afoul of the Alliance. Referenced in "Serenity".

Holder, *pr.n.* Slaver and silent partner who works with Wright. Appeared in "Shindig".

holo chandelier, *n.* Type of elaborate, high tech, expensive lamp that hangs from the ceiling. Holographic images create a sparkling effect to recreate a chandelier made out of glass or beads instead of holograms. A holo chandelier, which Kaylee refers to as a "chandelier", decorates the dance hall in "Shindig".

hologram, *n.* Three-dimensional image created with lasers. Holograms are

BELOW: Holograms, like the one you see pictured below, are widely used in medical equipment and scanners in 2517.

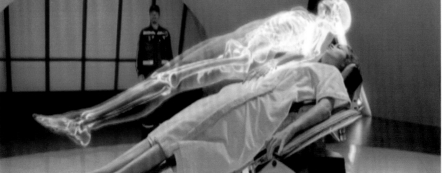

considered new tech in the 'Verse and are used in a variety of ways ranging from decorative to commercial use. Some holograms can move or be affected by touch.

holopool, *n.* Three-dimensional recreation of the game of bar pool. Holopool incorporates holographic images that are touch-sensitive. Malcolm Reynolds and Jayne Cobb play a glitchy game of holopool against a pair of slavers on the planet Santo at the beginning of "Shindig".

holster, *n.* 1. Firearm casing, typically made from leather, that's attached to a belt or strap. May be worn openly or beneath clothing. Mal and Zoë both wear holsters. *v.* 2. Place a gun into its protective casing, e.g. "Holster that firearm!"

homestead, *n.* Synonym for home. Commonly used by ranchers and farmers to refer to their main house and all their land.

Horowitz, *pr.n.* Middleman Captain Reynolds has worked with in the past. A poor candidate to sell government-stamped goods to, because he's broke. Referenced in "Serenity".

Horseshoes or **Horseshoe Toss,** *pr.n.* Recreational game where horseshoes, which are u-shaped, are thrown at a pole or stake from a distance. The game is scored by how many shoes land around the pole. Played by the *Serenity* crew.

hot, *adj. sl.* Dangerous. Treacherous.

hotbox, *n.* Case designed using a conductive material, utilized to punish and torture thieves and trespassers. A heat source is applied to the base of the box which raises the temperature inside it. Prisoners inside the hotbox suffer from the effects of the heat and may be burned. Stitch Hessian was imprisoned in a hotbox in Canton in "Jaynestown".

LEFT: Zoë's Old West-inspired brown leather vest and holster, designed by Shawna Trpcic and artist Jonathan A. Logan.

"Command says it's too hot. They're pulling out. We're to lay down arms."

– Corporal Zoë Alleyne, "Serenity"

House Madrassa, *pr.n.* Companion training facility located on Sihnon. Inara Serra went to live here as a little girl. Nandi, from "Heart of Gold", was a former Companion from House Madrassa.

House Priestess, *pr.n.* Title for the Head Companion. An administrative facility to oversee all functions of a House in order to make sure it runs smoothly. It is a prestigious position that carries political weight within the government.

hovercraft, *n.* Generic name referring to a low-flying vehicle designed to travel over land and water. Most hovercraft have downward-facing engines that generate pressure, allowing them to travel on a cushion of air. Hovercraft include trains, personal-sized vehicles, shuttles, etc. and may travel at high speeds. Unlike ships, hovercraft are not typically built for spaceflight and can only operate within a planetary or lunar atmosphere.

hull-piercing, *adj.* Of an object, typically a projectile, that has the ability to damage the hull of a ship.

hump, *v. vul.* 1. Act of forcibly rubbing one's genitalia on an object or person, e.g. vigorous sex. *interj. vul.* 2. When used in the past tense, humped means hosed. Screwed. The worst kind of luck, e.g. "We're humped!"

hydraulics, *n.* Ship system concerned with feeding chemically based liquids, like oil or fuel, to another part or system on the ship. "Cutting the hydraulics" refers to cutting wires that are part of this system, which effectively shuts down another system or part.

hydrozapam, *n.* Medicine Simon Tam recommended the crew take from the medvault in "Ariel".

hypo, *adj. abbr.* Short for hypodermic.

hypo gun, *n.* Plunger designed to pierce the skin with a needle. Typically used to inject medicine or drugs into the body.

hypo kit, *n.* Medical equipment that includes a hypo gun, needles, and sterilization equipment.

Hypocrates or **Hippocrates,** *pr.n.* Ancient Greek philosopher. Referenced in "Objects in Space".

Did you run into problems with using the word "humped"?

Whedon: Never. I've always had it easy with language, because I'll always throw in a word that's not quite the word we're not supposed to use, but clearly means it. And I honestly don't think I ever had a language problem. I mean, I kept saying "rutting" all the time and "bunged", which if you really break it down, is even more impressive [laughs]. In the early days of *Buffy*, I used British terms. And on *Firefly*, I used British, but usually Elizabethan terms, or terms that were made up to be ever so slightly different, but never any that would actually raise alarms, because nobody actually really seemed to know what they meant. The one big restriction we had was we couldn't say anything actually really dirty in Chinese. Because they were like, "Mm, if this goes overseas, people will be able to understand what they're saying, so you can't cuss." Originally, we had them cussing like sailors in Chinese, but they were like, "No, you have to say something that can be understood [without offending speakers of Chinese]." And then we found, because Chinese is so short, basically, it's the opposite of German or Japanese – there are no syllables of any kind – that we have to write monologues just for somebody to have a few syllables. That was a problem.

OPPOSITE: Burgess's hovercraft, as seen in "Heart of Gold".

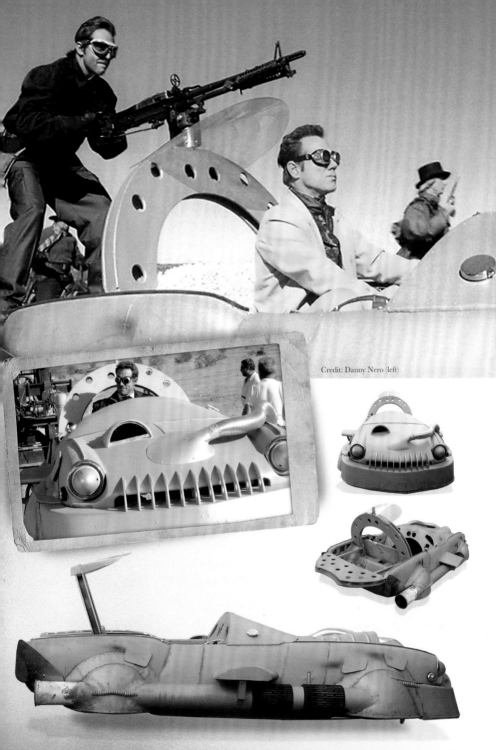

Credit: Danny Nero (left)

I.A.V. Dortmunder, pr.n. Name of the Alliance cruiser the *Serenity* crew was attempting to avoid in "Serenity".

I.A.V. Magellan, pr.n. Alliance cruiser patrolling the Red Sun System that patched up Shepherd Book's near-fatal gunshot wound in "Safe".

ident card, *n.* Piece of digitized paper that, when scanned, reveals the person's uniquely recorded history and identification according to Alliance records. Legal ident cards are required by law, and a person's access to equipment and vehicles is attached to the data on the card.

COMMANDER: How did this happen?

ZOË: He was –

MAL: Bystander in a gun fight. Back on Jiangyin. You can check. Not he nor any of ours were the aggressors.

COMMANDER: We aren't a medical facility, Captain. Our services aren't simply available to any—

BOOK: (weakly) Commander ... My ident card ... pocket ...

The Commander nods to the Ensign. He helps Book, comes up with an ident card ... a square of electronic paper. Mal and Zoë watch with interest

– weren't expecting this and don't quite know what to make of it.

The Ensign takes the card, slides it into a reading device (the size of a credit card imprinter) which overrides its privacy code, and takes in secured information on it. He hands it to the Commander. We can see information scrolling across the card. The Commander looks at it. Then, to the Ensign:

COMMANDER: (No nonsense) Get this man to the infirmary at once.
– "Safe"

ident scan, *n.* Results of the data recorded on an ident card, which reveal important details about a person's identity. Shepherd Book's ident scan saved his life in "Safe".

idjit, *n. sl.* Idiot. Fool.

illiterate, *adj.* 1. Without the ability to read or write. *adj.* 2. Of a person who cannot read or write. *n.* 3. Used as an insult to describe a person who acts as if they don't have the ability to think critically.

immunobooster, *n.* Drug engineered to improve immune system performance.

imprinted goods, *n. pl.* Cargo, usually stolen, that has been marked with a unique seal or symbol.

inbred, *adj.* 1. Characteristics related to offspring of family members who mate. *adj. vul.* 2. Of a person who is undesirable or lives in an isolated community outside the Central planets. Often used as a slight.

incense, *n.* Stick, bundle, or perfumed cone manufactured from ground herbs and flowers that is lit on fire to produce

LEFT: The details of Shepherd Book's ident card are unknown but it affords him respect and special privileges. BELOW: The Independent flag depicted in badge form.

smoke. Inara Serra burns incense in her shuttle. The use of incense is part of a Companion's customs, which ties into their Buddhist beliefs.

incubator, *n.* Controlled synthetic or biological closed environment used to grow biological cells, organs, or other tissues. In "The Message", Simon Tam discussed how Tracey Smith's torso was being used as an incubator for blastomeres.

indentured servitude, *n.* Indentured servitude is a common form of cheap labor that is often exploited by members of the Alliance ruling class. In exchange for the paying off of a debt, like passage on board a ship, poor colonists and settlers agree to work a certain number of years for the wealthier person who cleared their accounts. The Mudders on Higgins' Moon are an example of indentured servitude. They are too poor to leave the moon and are in a constant state of debt which, in turn, traps them in their circumstance with no way out.

Independent Faction, *pr.n.* Coalition of planets and moons in the Border and rim that fought for the right to remain independent from the Alliance in the Unification War that ended six years ago. While the Independents did have a military and some combined resources, the Alliance proved to be the mightier opponent due to its great wealth, higher numbers of military personnel, and the significant damage it caused

BELOW: Companions maintain rich traditions, such as the tea ceremony and the burning of incense. These are all expected aspects of a client's experience with a Companion, and are part of Companions' religious heritage.

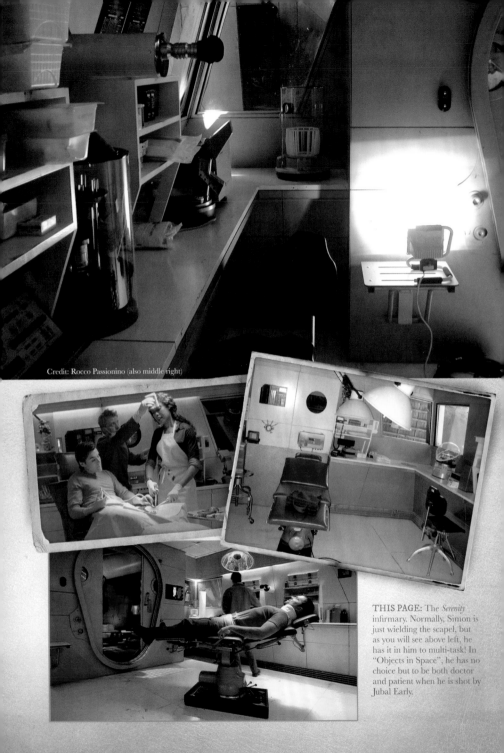

Credit: Rocco Passionino (also middle right)

THIS PAGE: The *Serenity* infirmary. Normally, Simon is just wielding the scapel, but as you will see above left, he has it in him to multi-task! In "Objects in Space", he has no choice but to be both doctor and patient when he is shot by Jubal Early.

on the field of battle to the Independents and their homes. In a post-Unification War environment, Independent Faction veterans have been decimated by the heavy losses they sustained and many choose to abandon civilization altogether. Malcolm Reynolds and Zoë Alleyne Washburne are the only two confirmed members of the Independent Faction on board *Serenity*.

infirmary, *n.* Specially designed, sterile room in a ship assigned to a medic or doctor in order to serve the crew's medical needs. Typically, a ship's infirmary has less supplies than a hospital would, but more than an isolated settlement.

inter-engine fermentation system, *n.* Elaborate system designed to quickly produce cheap alcohol by speeding up the fermentation process.

interface, *adj.* Of the ability to program a console, programmable pad, or similar equipment, e.g. "Interface strike-plate".

interplanetary, *adj.* Across all planets, regardless of location in the 'Verse.

interplanetary borders, *n. pl.* Perimeters that designate the distance between the celestial bodies that are located in every system. These key boundaries are used to plot ship trajectories, were clearly identified following the end of the Unification War, and are now controlled by the Anglo-Sino Alliance.

Interpol, *pr.n. abbr.* The Interplanetary Police.

"Put a bulletin out on the Cortex, and flag Interpol: a Firefly with possible stolen goods aboard."

– Captain, *I.A.V. Dortmunder*, "Serenity"

Isis Canyon, *pr.n.* Desolate, uninhabited stretch of desert on Bellerophon. Mal was left naked and stranded in Isis Canyon, and Saffron was captured in a trash bin here by Inara during "Trash".

isoprovalyn, *n.* Common pharmaceutical drug used to boost a patient's immune system. Valuable on the black market.

Ita, *pr.n.* Moon orbiting Whittier, a planet in the rim's Kalidasa System. The crew of the *S.S. Walden* left a salvage mission here before they encountered Mal in "Out of Gas".

IV, *n. abbrev.* Intravenous. An IV is a tube connected to fluids that's inserted into a patient's vein.

ABOVE: Mal is left exposed in the harsh conditions of Isis Canyon on Bellerophon, much to the delight of some of the Captain's Browncoat admirers!

jabber, *v.* 1. Speak enthusiastically and rapidly. Blather on and on, but talking so fast that it doesn't make any sense. *n* 2. Incoherent string of words spoken in rapid succession, e.g. "Can you slow it down some? Can't make heads or tails of your jabber."

Jacks, *pr.n.* Game Kaylee and River played in "Objects in Space". There are many variations on this game, but the core concept involves bouncing a rubber ball on a flat surface and picking up jacks in between bounces.

jake, *adj. sl.* Fine. O.K. Satisfactory, e.g. "Everything's jake by me."

Jayne Day, *pr.n.* A fake holiday to celebrate Jayne Cobb, thereby drawing the Mudders and the people of Canton out of the factory. This ruse was orchestrated by Mal to smuggle mud back onto *Serenity*. Occurred in "Jaynestown."

jerry-rig or **jury rig,** *v.* Throw together technical components in order to create a temporary solution to fix an existing part or system. *adj.* 2. Of an object that's produced haphazardly to create a temporary result, like the jerry-rigged Crybaby.

Jiangyin, *pr.n.* Planet in the Red Sun System. The primary location where the episode "Safe" took place.

Johan, *pr.n.* Law official who is friends with Gabriel Tam. According to Gabriel, he took bribes and would wipe Simon's arrest record clean. Simon was arrested during a vice unit raid in the red light district. He refused Gabriel's offer to contact Johan. Referred to in "Safe".

John Thomas, *pr.n. sl.* Slang for penis. The origin of the name refers to the well-endowed Sir John Thomas, who was Lady Chatterley's lover in the nineteenth century on Earth-That-Was.

Judgement Day, *pr.n.* Armageddon. The apocalypse as written in the Bible.

junker, *n. sl.* Crappy ship. Piece of trash. Commander Harken called *Serenity* a junker in front of Kaylee in "Bushwhacked".

BELOW: Kaylee and River play a game of Jacks during "Objects in Space".

JAYNESTOWN

CANTON

ABOVE: Jayne Day might have been a fake holiday, but the Hero of Canton's statue in his

K

ABOVE: A lively kabuki performance transfixes passers-by in Eavesdown Docks.

BELOW: QMx's double-sided Map of the 'Verse explores planets as far out as the rim, including the Kalidasa System.

kabuki, *n.* Ancient Japanese theatrical performance involving heavily made up actors who sing, mime, and use exaggerated gestures and props, like wooden swords, to tell a story. Kabuki actors appeared at Eavesdown Docks in "Serenity".

Kalidasa System, *pr.n.* Planetary system on the rim that includes worlds like Beaumonde, Newhall, and Beylix.

keel, *n.* Fin-like part on naval vessels that extends from the boat for added control/stability.

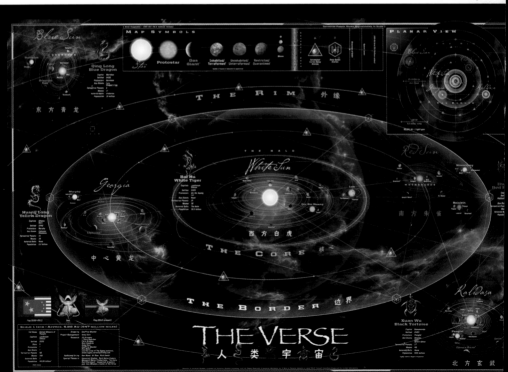

Credit: Danny Nero

RIGHT: Burgess's ally Kozick, seen here at his mounted gun, is killed by Jayne in the "Heart of Gold" firefight.

keelhaul, *v.* Severe punishment for sailors. May result in death. Involves tying the sailor to the keel while the ship is moving.

Keene, *pr.n.* Military police officer under Commander Harken in "Bushwhacked".

Kessler, *pr.n.* Middleman Captain Reynolds was supposed to meet in Canton. He was caught stealing by the foreman and his prods. For his crime, his limbs were cut off and he was thrown into a bog. An unidentified well-dressed man then met with Mal, assuring him that the stolen mud was safe in "Kessler's hiding place".

keycard, *n.* Small piece of plastic coded with data that, when scanned, will provide access to a device or area.

kiss the dirt, *id.* Fall to the ground hard after being injured or shot, possibly dead.

klaxon, *n.* Emergency horn that blasts a loud noise. Most ships are equipped with this warning signal, and they are programmed to go off when key systems or parts fail.

Kowlan fed base, *pr.n. abbr.* Kowlan federal base. During "Safe", Badger requested that the smuggled loot be dropped off here with his men. This infers that Badger has ties to law enforcement who accept bribes.

Kozick, *pr.n.* Rance Burgess's ally who manned a mounted gun in the big showdown during "Heart of Gold".

Kumamota, Q., R.N., *pr.n.* Zoë's E.M.T. alias in "Ariel".

laconic, *adj.* Pertains to the use of few words. Applies to a succinct style of writing or speech, e.g. "I appreciate your laconic message. I like how you get to the point."

lady, *n. fem.* 1. Polite salutation for woman. *n. fem.* 2. High class socialite or well-mannered woman with regal bearing, like a Companion. *n. fem. uc.* 3. Title of nobility, e.g. "Introducing Lord and Lady Stowe."

lambie-toes, *n. pl. sl.* Literally, lamb toes. Affectionate term describing a lover of a sweet nature.

land-lock, *n.* Government-sanctioned code used to disable a ship's computer to prevent it from taking off. Well-governed moons, like Higgins' Moon, and civilized planets use land-locks to prevent criminals and fugitives from escaping.

HIGGINS: You did WHAT!?

FESS: I sent an override to Port Control. Lifted the land-lock on *Serenity*.

HIGGINS: I ought to tear that smile off your head! How dare you defy me! You – You –

FESS: You wanted to make a man of me, Dad. I guess it worked.

– "Jaynestown"

ABOVE: Burgess's laser gun, as seen in "Heart of Gold". Unlike a lot of *Firefly* props, this one is actually a real sci-fi raygun, but its battery goes flat at the crucial moment - proof that you shouldn't blindly trust in technology, even on a sci-fi show!

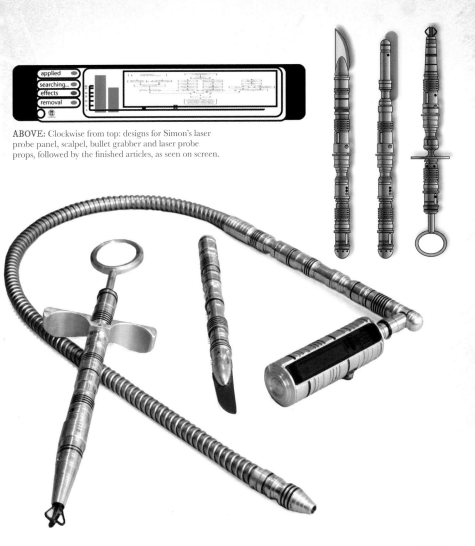

ABOVE: Clockwise from top: designs for Simon's laser probe panel, scalpel, bullet grabber and laser probe props, followed by the finished articles, as seen on screen.

LaRue, Kiki, R.N., *pr.n.* Name printed on an E.M.T. badge. The alias used by Jayne Cobb in "Ariel".

laser gun, *n.* A "silk trigger active return bolt laser" firearm owned by Rance Burgess in "Heart of Gold".

laser probe, *n.* Exploratory medical instrument used in surgery.

laser saw, *n.* Surgical instrument involving the use of lasers used to cut bone and tissue.

ABOVE: The laser probe panel was back-lit to give it a more authentic feel on screen.

The mark's name is Durran Haymer. Maybe one of the biggest collectors of Earth-That-Was artifacts in the Verse. Guy's got warehouses full of stuff. But his prize piece is sitting in this parlor — an antiquity of unspeakable value: the Lassiter. The original hand-held laser pistol. One of only two known to still exist. The forerunner of all modern technology. Haymer got lucky, picked it up during the war for nothing. — Saffron, "Trash"

mall for travelers. Offers entertainment, food, supplies, and Alliance-sanctioned services. Appeared in "The Message".

Liberty Hammer, *pr.n.* Pistol Malcolm Reynolds uses.

lieutenant, *n.* 1. Military rank. Used by the Independent Faction in the Unification War. Ranked above a corporal and a sergeant. *n.* 2. Rank in law enforcement. Captain of a police force. *pr.n. uc.* 3. Title referring to rank held, e.g. Lieutenant Womack, Lieutenant Baker.

lifeboat, *n.* On a spaceship, an emergency shuttle.

lip ferret, *n. masc. sl.* Overgrown moustache or unkempt handlebar moustache.

literacy, *n.* Knowledge related to the act of reading and writing language. In the 'Verse, literacy is not a guarantee and varies widely. A person's ability to read and write is primarily shaped by economic and geographical factors. In general, citizens who grow up in the White Sun System have better educational opportunities than anyone else in the 'Verse. Jayne makes fun of Simon for his speech in "Jaynestown" when he calls him Little Miss Big Words.

lobotomy, *n.* Brain operation to lessen a patient's psychological suffering that

Lassiter, *pr.n.* Earth-That-Was artifact and the target of the heist in "Trash".

latrine, *n.* Communal toilet. Usually small, like an outhouse. Not large enough to contain a bathtub or shower.

lawman, *n. sl. masc.* Nickname for a male sheriff, marshall, deputy, or other legal representative who upholds the law by pursuing all types of criminals.

layer cake dress, *n.* Style of gown that's sewn with overlapping panels of material draped over a hoopskirt to resemble a layer cake. Kaylee wore (and got to keep) a pink-and-white layer cake dress in "Shindig".

Li Shen's Space Bazaar, *pr.n.* Mobile space station that serves as a floating shopping

ABOVE: Mal wields the Liberty Hammer. The pistol was created by LA prop shop Applied Effects for the show and built on an existing live-fire revolver.

OPPOSITE: Kaylee wears a layer cake dress in "Shindig".

ABOVE: These triangular badges were worn by Independent soldiers during the Unification War. The rank shown here is that of lieutenant.

"You been birddoggin' this township a while now, and they wouldn't mind a corpse of you. Now you could luxuriate in a nice jail cell but if your hand touches metal, I swear by my pretty floral bonnet I will end you." – Malcolm Reynolds, "Our Mrs Reynolds"

RIGHT: Lugar owned by Inara Serra.

LEFT: The social elite wear sashes like this one to indicate the title of lordhood that was bestowed upon them.

involves severing the connection to the pre-frontal lobe. Considered barbaric.

local pipeline, *n. id.* Communication channels that are concentrated in a nearby area. May refer to people or technology.

lock-down or **lock down,** *v.* 1. On a ship, shutting doors to seal off areas of the ship in progression. *n.* 2. State of a ship that's been locked down.

Londinium, *pr.n.* Planet second-closest to Bai Hu, the White Sun at the heart of the system. It is one of two capital planets, and is the primary location of parliament, where the Anglo-Sino Alliance government conducts its business. Mal refers to the "king of all Londinium" in "Serenity".

longblade, *n. sl.* Sword or rapier.

lordhood, *n. masc.* Title given to nobility. Nobles wear sashes to indicate their station at formal events, like the party in "Shindig".

luck, *n.* Chance. Mystical or religious forces that shape circumstances. Something the *Serenity* crew always seems to be on the losing side of.

Lucy, *pr.n.* Prostitute in the Heart of Gold. She sang at Nandi's funeral.

Lugar or **Luger,** *pr.n.* Manufacturer of Inara Serra's pistol in "Trash". A heavily-modified version of a WWII pistol from Earth-That-Was known as a Ruger Mk II, which Mal carries during "Heart of Gold".

Lund, *pr.n.* Tried-and-true fan of the Alliance who got drunk and mouthed off to Mal about the Independents on Unification Day.

luxuriate, *v.* Relax. Indulge oneself.

luxury liner, *n.* Spaceship designed to cater to wealthy clientele by providing a lavish, relaxing experience. The twenty-sixth-century equivalent of a cruise ship.

M.D., *n. abbr.* Short for medical doctor.

M.P., *n. abbr.* Short for military police.

mag-drop, *n.* Type of concussive depth charge designed to disable a ship's electrical system. Fries a ship's electronics. Used in "The Message" by Lieutenant Womack.

magnetic grappler, *n.* Type of hook that connects one ship to another, potentially damaging the hull of the targeted ship. Commonly used by Reavers.

maiden house, *n. fem.* Residential building in the Triumph Settlement containing female virgins waiting to be married. The single women who occupy the maiden house are commodities given to men in exchange for much-needed supplies.

main, *n.* Primary or most important, e.g. "the main engine".

man, *adj.* 1. Number of passengers or pilots a ship can hold, regardless of gender, e.g. "one-man fighter". *v.* 2. Stand in position to operate a piece of equipment, e.g. "Man that station!" *n. abbr.* 3. Short for humanity. *n. sing.* 4. Member of the *homo sapiens* species. *n. masc.* 5. Referring to a human male. *interj.* 6. Spoken to relay a strong emotion like surprise, amazement, or disgust, e.g. "Man oh man!"

Mandarin Chinese, *pr.n.* Mandarin Chinese is the Alliance's official tongue and the primary language used in printed

"I lived my life in the maiden house, waiting to be married off for trade. I seen my sistren paired off with ugly men, vicious or blubberous, men with appetites too unseemly to speak on."

– Saffron, "Our Mrs Reynolds"

ABOVE: Inara practises calligraphy in "Bushwhacked" (top) and a sign from "Shindig" (bottom) informs patrons that management will not be held responsible for flickering holopool balls.

ABOVE: Mal and Saffron's marriage ceremony.
RIGHT: River sketches matroyshka dolls.

materials. As such, it's a common tongue that's understood throughout the 'Verse.

Mare's Leg or **Mare's Laig,** *pr.n.* Pet name for the customized rifle used by Zoë Alleyne Washburne. Her lever-action rifle has a shortened barrel and its butt-stock has been trimmed down. The original manufacturer is the legendary Winchester.

marriage, *n.* Like divorce, marriage customs and how the couple is registered legally vary widely throughout the 'Verse. In "Our Mrs Reynolds", Mal is thought to be legally married to Saffron. Yolanda/Saffron/Bridget exploited marriage customs in order to con her husbands.

math, *n.* 1. Numerical computations. *n. sl.* 2. Private Cortex number. *n. sl.* 3. Logic. Rationale, e.g. "What's the math on that?"

mathematics, *n.* Field of study encompassing geometry, calculus, algebra, and basic arithmetic. Crucial for studying or applying aeronautics to flight trajectories.

matryoshka doll or **Russian nesting doll,** *n.* Sequence of colorful, oval dolls with a flat bottom in variable sizes that are designed to fit together from the smallest to the largest. River draws matryoshka dolls at the end of "Ariel".

Maynard, *pr.n.* The Councilor's son. Referenced in an unaired scene during "War Stories".

McGinnis, Agent, *pr.n.* Commanding officer who negotiated with Jayne Cobb to capture Simon and River Tam in "Ariel". He was killed by the enigmatic hands of blue.

ABOVE: Simon at work in the infirmary in "Bushwhacked".

Meadows, *pr.n.* Jayne Cobb's biggest fan in "Jaynestown". He later sacrificed himself so his hero could live.

Medacad, *pr.n.* The Medacad is a prestigious school found in the Central planets where aspiring doctors and surgeons go to study. Simon Tam studied at a Medacad on Osiris.

medic, *n.* Nurse or medical technician. Military term that has since fallen into common use.

Medical Elect, *pr.n.* Highest-ranking position in a hospital. This person is proficient in medicine, oversees all administrative functions, and reports to the Alliance.

medicine, *n.* 1. Field of study related to human health. *n.* 2. Pharmaceutical or natural drugs designed to heal or affect the body so it can be healed.

med-kit, *n.* Doctor's case filled with medicine, tools, and supplies like weaves.

medvault, *n.* Secure storage room in a hospital where medicine is kept.

meet'cha, *abbr. sl.* Short for "meet you", e.g. "Pleased to meet'cha."

mercenary, *n.* Gun-for-hire whose primary motivation is to get paid.

metal, *n. sl.* Gun or pistol. Refers to the weapon's casing.

middleman, *n. masc.* Go-between that takes illegal goods or smuggled cargo and sells them for a cut of the profits. Bolles, on Ezra, was a middleman.

military rank, *n.* System of hierarchical positions to denote importance and responsibility. Varies based on type of military operation. Examples of titles include: Commander, Sergeant, Lieutenant, Corporal, and Private.

milk run, *n. sl.* 1. Supply route that includes stops for multiple buyers. *n. sl.* 2. An easy job, task, or mission.

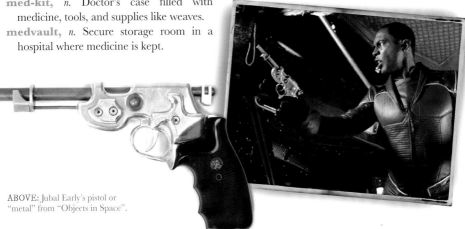

ABOVE: Jubal Early's pistol or "metal" from "Objects in Space".

ABOVE: Wash attempts to repair and reprogram a salvaged motherboard in "Ariel".

ABOVE: Banning Miller tries to ridicule Kaylee at the society dance in "Shindig" before she gets her just desserts at the hands of Kaylee's noble admirer Murphy.

Miller, Banning, *pr.n.* Snooty socialite who attempted to make fun of Kaylee for not having a seamstress in "Shindig".

miner, *n.* Person who drills into a celestial body to mine underground for minerals and other resources. Mining occurs on the Border planets, like Regina.

mite, *adj. sl.* Diminutive size. Small.

mole, *n. sl.* Member of a criminal or legal organization who infiltrates an enemy by going undercover and fulfilling orders. Objectives vary broadly. In "Serenity", Lawrence Dobson was an Alliance mole masquerading as a friendly, paying passenger.

moneybag, *n.* For a bank, a thick, canvas bag that contains currency. For a smuggler or thief, any bag that contains payment for illicit goods or services from another party.

Monty, *pr.n.* Mal and Zoë's war buddy who shaved off his beard for his new bride, Bridget. Their wedded bliss was to be short-lived as Bridget turned out to be Saffron in "Trash".

moon, *n.* 1. Celestial body that orbits a planet. *n.* 2. *Serenity*'s bulbous tail end, the sight another ship would see as she flies away.

moon brain, *n. sl.* Babbling idiot or fool. Lunatic. Durran Haymer referred to himself as a moon brain after he saw his missing wife, Yolanda, in "Trash".

mortar, *n.* Military weapon designed to fire missiles or other projectile weapons.

motherboard, *n.* Primary set of computerized circuits wired into a board. A motherboard is an important component in automated and programmable devices.

motivator, *n.* Ship part. Referenced at the end of "Trash".

mud bog, *n.* Wetland where mud is difficult to extract due to an unusually high water content. On Canton, where the foreman and his prods dump dismembered corpses in "Jaynestown."

Mudders, *pr.n. sl.* Indentured workers who occupy Canton and harvest clay and mud for Canton Mudworks, which is owned by Magistrate Higgins. The Mudders were at odds with their employer, and believed that Jayne Cobb was their savior in "Jaynestown".

Mudders' Milk, *pr.n.* Nutrient-rich, alcoholic liquid bread provided to the mud workers.

JAYNE: Mmm. They call it Mudders' Milk. All the protein, vitamins and carbs of your grandma's best turkey dinner, plus fifteen percent alcohol.

WASH: It's horrific!

SIMON: Worked for the Egyptians.

JAYNE: What's that?

SIMON: The ancient Egyptians, back on Earth-That-Was. It's not so different from the ancestral form of beer they fed to the slaves who built their pyramids. Liquid bread. Kept them from starving, and knocked them out at night, so they wouldn't be inclined to insurrection.

– "Jaynestown"

Mudville, *n. sl.* Alternate name for Canton on Higgins' Moon.

Mule, *pr.n. sl.* 1. Name of the *Serenity* crew's four-wheel all-terrain vehicle. The Mule carries cargo to and from the ship. *n. lc. vul.* 2. Person who is stuffed with an illegal substance, like drugs or blastomeres, hired or forced into servitude by a crime boss or syndicate.

Murphy, *pr.n.* Elderly gentleman who put Banning Miller in her place and entertained Kaylee in "Shindig".

mutation, *n.* Forced or accidental change in animal or human DNA that creates the appearance of an unusual trait with physical characteristics. Simon explained how the alien in Li Shen's Space Bazaar was a mutated cow fetus in "The Message".

Mylar, *pr.n.* Brand of thin reflective film used for insulation. The Heart of Gold located on Deadwood was covered with Mylar.

ABOVE: A bloody moneybag once possessed by the Grange brothers in "Safe". The money was to be used to pay Mal off for the illegal cattle he transported to Jiangyin. The currency includes untraceable platinum coins.

Nandi, *pr.n.* Former Companion of House Madrassa who flew to Deadwood and carved out a piece of territory for herself. Ran a whorehouse called the Heart of Gold and, after running into problems with Rance Burgess and his men, called Inara for help. Appeared in "Heart of Gold". She is now deceased.

INARA: It sounds like something this crew can handle. I can't guarantee they'll handle it particularly well but ...

NANDI: If they've got guns and brains at all ...

INARA: They've got guns.

– "Heart of Gold"

navcom, *n.* Short for navigational computer. An important ship part responsible for plotting flight paths, maintaining a ship's trajectory, identifying celestial bodies, spotting oncoming vessels, etc.

nekked, *adj. sl.* Alternate spelling and rustic pronunciation of the word "naked". Doesn't have any clothes on. Birthday suit.

neural imager, *n.* High tech diagnostic equipment that allows a medical technician or doctor to create a holographic image of a patient's brain.

New Canaan brandy, *pr.n.* Rare, premium spirit distilled on the planet New Canaan in the Blue Sun System. Gabriel Tam bought Simon a bottle of aged New Canaan brandy in the unaired script for "Safe".

New Dunsmuir, *pr.n.* City located on

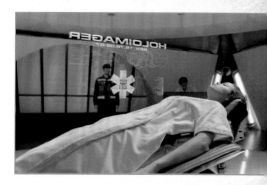

the planet Beaumonde in the Kalidasa System. Inara Serra has clients that live here. Referred to in "Our Mrs Reynolds".

New Kasmir or **New Kashmir,** *pr.n.* Rim planet in the Kalidasa System. Sergeant Malcolm Reynolds and Corporal Zoë Alleyne fought here during the Unification War in a winter campaign.

New Melbourne, *pr.n.* Planet in the Red Sun System known for its fisheries and oceans. A popular destination for inhabitants of the Border planets and rim.

new tech, *n.* Colloquial phrase referring to cutting-edge technology, tested and untested, commonly found in the Core. May refer to diagnostic systems, computer equipment, vehicles, and a wide range of other devices and inventions. New tech surpasses what most people can afford outside of the Central planets; it is very expensive. Rance Burgess, from "Heart of Gold", is an example of someone who sought new tech to impress the locals and solidify his position. His laser gun and hovercar are considered new tech. As the failure of his gun shows, however, new tech isn't always guaranteed to work until it's been through proper testing.

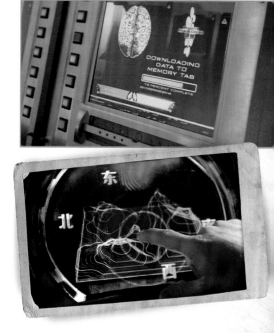

Newhall, *pr.n.* Planet in the Kalidasa System. The colonists found dead in "Bushwhacked" after their ship had been hit by Reavers were headed to Newhall for the first time.

Ng-Ka-Pei, *pr.n.* Commonly found brand of beer.

Niska, Adelai, *pr.n.* Crime boss of a far-reaching syndicate who lives in a space station orbiting Ezra in the Georgia System. He has a collection of Earth-That-Was artifacts and puts on the pretense that he is loyal to his family. The kingpin has a

strong footing in the Georgia System and has bribed the World Council on Ezra to look the other way. His Slavic accent reflects that he's a native speaker of an Eastern European language that survived the trip from Earth-That-Was. Appeared in "The Train Job" and "War Stories".

NISKA: Oh, you do not like I kill this man?

MAL: Oh no, I'm sure he was a very ... bad person.

NISKA: My wife's nephew. At dinner I am getting an earful. There is no way out of that.

– "The Train Job"

no-good reptile, *n. id.* Person who is a backstabber or evil in some fashion, like the snake in the Garden of Eden. Stitch Hessian refers to Jayne as a no-good reptile in "Jaynestown".

nonsensical, *adj.* 1. Illogical. Doesn't have any real meaning. The facts don't add up. *adj.* 2. Foolish and impractical. Absurd. Ridiculous.

nubile, *adj. fem.* Traits of a young, sexually attractive female.

ABOVE: Adelai Niska is the head of a criminal syndicate. He owns a Skyplex which orbits the planet Ezra, and his methods of ensuring he gets what he wants include intimidation and torture.

Obrin, Colonel, *pr.n.* Fought with Sergeant Reynolds, Corporal Alleyne, and Private Smith in the Unification War. Mal referred to him fondly in "The Message" and recalled how Tracey played a joke on him by cutting off his prized moustache.

> *"When you can't run, you crawl ... and when you can't crawl, when you can't do that – you find someone to carry you."*
>
> – Tracey Smith, "The Message"

off your nut, *id.* Insult thrown at a speaker who has said something so bizarre that that person must be insane.

off-planet, *adj.* Of an event, object, person, or location that is on another planet/moon.

old saying, *n.* Bit of wisdom or phrase with emotional or cultural weight, e.g. the motto repeated by Tracey Smith in "The Message".

ore processors, *n. pl.* Complex, intricate machines used in mining to extract and process ore from deep underground. Referenced in "The Train Job".

Osiris, *pr.n.* Planet in the White Sun System. Simon and River Tam's homeworld.

BELOW: The planet Osiris, and the Tam family home, is seen through Simon's flashback scenes in "Safe".

palaver, *v.* Chit-chat or talk idly for an extended period of time. An overly long discussion, e.g. "Sorry I'm late. We palavered for a good while."

Palestinian Somersault, *pr.n.* Complex acrobatic movement that contorts the body in a unique, seductive way to attract a member of the opposite sex. The Palestinian Somersault is a trick that Helen performed in "Heart of Gold".

pantywaist, *n. fem. sl.* Insult directed at a feeble, overly sensitive man. Someone with a weak constitution who cries at the drop of a hat.

Paquin, *pr.n.* Planet in the Red Sun System. It held a job opportunity for the *Serenity* crew. Referenced in "Out of Gas".

Paradiso, *pr.n.* Mining town located on the planet Regina in the Georgia System. Primary location of the episode "Safe".

Paragon, *pr.n.* Ship docked at Eavesdown Docks on Persephone in "Serenity". Kaylee points out its flaws to Shepherd Book.

Parth, *pr.n.* Third moon of Bellerophon in the White Sun System. The alleged location where Yolanda Haymer had been imprisoned for the past six years. Referred to in "Trash".

Pasceline D or **Pescaline D,** *pr.n.* Remedy manufactured to relieve the symptoms of and/or possibly cure the disease called "Bowden's Malady". This medicine is freely supplied by the Alliance to Regina's residents as a form of restitution

ABOVE: The town of Paradiso, located on the planet Regina in the Georgia System.

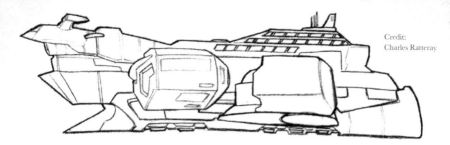

ABOVE: Design by Charles Ratteray for the *Paragon* ship, as seen in Eavesdown Docks in "Serenity".

Credit:
Charles Ratteray

for the medical problems caused by the terraforming process.

passel, *n.* Large group of people. A crowd or a pack, e.g. "Looks like we've got a passel of Mudders who're anxious to celebrate Jayne Day."**petty,** *adj.* Of trivial or minor importance. Lesser. Occasionally used as a slight, e.g. "petty thief" or "petty crime".

passenger dorm, *n.* Area of rooms on a ship designed for crewmembers and travelers. Several rooms, which are also referred to as "bunks", make up this section of the ship.

Patience, *pr.n.* Potential buyer of Alliance-stamped cargo who aspires to become a moon boss. Lives on Whitefall. Appeared in "Serenity". She and Mal have a history.

Patron, *pr.n.* Opportunistic ruler of an isolated religious community on Jiangyin. According to River, he killed the former Patron to become the new leader. Agrees to burning River Tam at the stake for crimes of witchcraft in "Safe".

patsy, *n.* Stooge. Person who's easily conned, cheated, or manipulated. Takes the fall for others' crimes.

pecker, *n. masc. sl. vul.* 1. Term for penis. *n. masc. sl. vul.* 2. Arrogant, unlikeable male. A dick, e.g. "That pecker should've kept his mouth shut."

Pendy, Deputy, *pr.n.* Law official who assists Sheriff Bourne and who appeared in "The Train Job". She worked with Bourne to uncover the

ABOVE: The Patron of Jiangyin orders River to be burned at the stake as a witch after she reads his mind and starts revealing his secret.

ABOVE: Despite its location, Persephone is a Core planet. Its cities, like Eavesdown Docks, have futuristic skyscrapers and technology.

people responsible for stealing the miners' medicine.

Persephone, *pr.n.* Planet in the Core. Persephone lies near the boundary of the White Sun System. The *Serenity* crew frequently visits this planet.

personal log, *n.* Handwritten or digital journal kept by a ship's captain to record the events that happen on a vessel. Referred to in "Bushwhacked".

personnel carrier, *n.* Type of military vessel used to transport soldiers and officers. Often used in wartime situations.

Petaline, *pr.n.* Pregnant prostitute whose son is at the center of the "Heart of Gold" episode. After Nandi's death, she takes over the brothel.

Pierre, *pr.n.* Merchant of fine liquors and liqueurs who acquired a bottle of aged New Caanan brandy for Gabriel Tam.

pinch, *v. sl.* Arrest by officers of the law, e.g. "I almost got pinched on Ariel."

pin-lock, *n.* Two-part mechanism designed to fasten objects together with a pin inserted through holes at the top.

pisspot, *n.* 1. Bowl used to urinate into. *n. vul.* 2. Drunk. Used as an insult.

"I said, you're a coward and a pisspot. Now what're you gonna do about it?"

– Lund, "The Train Job"

pistola, *n. sl.* Colloquial use of pistol. Handgun.

plasmatics, *n.* 1. Field of study that focuses on synthetic and natural plasma. *n.* 2. Medical equipment designed to perform functions related to plasmatics.

plastic dinosaurs, *n. pl.* Colorful plastic toys shaped like prehistoric creatures. Enjoyed by Wash in "Serenity".

plating, *n.* Refers to the material used to make a spaceship's hull.

platinum, *n.* Form of currency used in the Border planets. Patience arranged to buy Mal's cargo for 200 platinum in "Serenity".

police, *n.* Local officers assigned to a municipality or town. Unlike other law officials, the police typically remain within a designated area to keep the peace. Federal marshalls and Alliance agents outrank the police, who must step aside when required.

port, *n.* 1. Designated spot to land a ship. *n.* 2. Direction used in flight and sailing to mark a bearing toward the left, e.g. "hard to port". *adj.* 3. Pertaining to the left side, or left-handed control or object, e.g. "The port catalyzer is on the left."

Port Control, *pr.n.* Local authority that monitors landings and takeoffs on a spaceport. The Port Control works with law enforcement and will call them in if needed. It is also a government entity and reports to a local ruler. The Port Control on Higgins' Moon answered to Magistrate and Fess Higgins.

port jet control, *n.* Ship's mechanism that operates the left-hand side jet.

portable keyboard, *n.* Mechanical device that can reprogram automated or programmable systems. Used by Kaylee in "Trash".

post holer, *n.* Farming equipment used to dig holes for posts. Kaylee explains what this is to Simon in "Safe".

LEFT: A selection of Wash's favorite dinosaurs.

post-op, *n. abbr.* Relates to the period following an operation.

pot lickings, *n. pl. sl.* Few remaining morsels of a meal that are so meager they can't be considered scraps or leftovers.

prairie harpy, *n. fem.* Filthy, foul woman who makes her home in a field of tall grasses. Used as an insult for women and girls who live on a Border planet.

prayer, *n.* Act of faith. An important part of Shepherd Book's religious practice.

Preacher, *pr.n.* Alternate title for a Shepherd.

ZOË: Preacher, don't the bible got some pretty specific things to say about killing?

BOOK: Quite specific. It is, however, somewhat fuzzier on the subject of kneecaps.

– "War Stories"

prefect, *n.* Type of Alliance government official. Similar to the role of a magistrate.

press regulator, *n.* Control pad accessed through a panel on the ship's engine.

pressure catch, *n.* Type of locking mechanism that acts as a switch. When

attached to a door, it is typically activated by the act of opening or closing the door.

primary, *adj.* First or main. Used to identify key systems in a complex mechanical or technical invention, like a ship.

private, *n.* Bottom rung in the Independent Faction's military.

prod, *n.* Title for a middle-ranked manager who directly oversees production for Canton Mudworks on Higgins' Moon.

propoxin, *n.* Medicine named by Simon Tam in "Ariel". Located in the medvault at

BELOW: Shepherd Book prays for infirmary patient Kaylee in "Serenity".

BELOW: Simon's birthday cake is formed out of chocolate-flavored protein in "Out of Gas".

St Lucy's and valuable on the black market.

protein, *n.* Synthetically and organically produced nutrient that is a common foodstuff, and necessary for survival. Because protein is cheap to produce and has a long shelf life, the Alliance engineered protein bars that were destined for colonists in the Border and rim. Available in powder and solid form in a rainbow of colors and flavors. Simon Tam's birthday cake was made out of protein in "Out of Gas".

proto-comatose, *n.* False state of unconsciousness caused by medicines or medical procedures.

protostar, *n.* Gas giant or brown dwarf that has been helioformed and turned into a sun. Each planetary system in the 'Verse has one or more protostars.

proximity alert, *n.* Ship alarm that is triggered when another object or vehicle approaches the hull. Warns pilots of oncoming ships.

psychic, *adj.* 1. Of a preternatural ability. *n.* 2. Person who displays superhuman mental abilities like the ability to move objects with the mind or read people's thoughts. Readers are a type of psychic that display telepathic abilities. *Serenity* crewmemember River Tam appears to be psychic.

psychotic, *adj.* Of a psychosis, a state of mental illness.

ABOVE: Zoë searches the St Lucy's medical stores for vital prescription drugs like propoxin, which can be resold on the black market for a tidy profit.

WASH: Psychic, though? That sounds like something out of science fiction!
ZOË: You live in a spaceship, dear.
– "Objects in Space"

puddle of piss, *n. vul.* Slang for an object, person, or vehicle that is so worthless, it's akin to human waste.

pulmonary stimulators, *n. pl.* Medical equipment designed to send an electrical charge to the heart in order to reset it or bring the heart rate up.

purplebelly, *n. sl.* Derogatory term for Alliance soldiers and loyalists. Used as an insult.

quadrant, *n.* Large section of space or a designated area. Quadrants are marked by the interplanetary borders within a system.

quim, *n. fem. vul.* Derogatory term for vagina that dates back to the Victorian era. Used as an insult.

it. This was Elder Gommen's gift to Jayne Cobb in "Our Mrs Reynolds".

JAYNE: All I got was this dumb-ass stick that sounds like it's raining. How come you got a wife?
MAL: I didn't. (To Saffron) We ain't married.
— "Our Mrs Reynolds"

radar screen, *n.* Part of the computer console that displays the visual data recorded by a radar scan. Allows pilots to visually notice oncoming ships, missiles, or other celestial objects. The radar screen and proximity alert work in tandem with one another.

radio earwig, *n.* Audio-communications device that allows a listener to hear over a radio frequency. Mal wore an earwig frequently to communicate with the *Serenity* crew when he was not on board.

rainstick, *n.* Ancient invention from Earth-That-Was that may have originated in Central or South America. A rainstick is a tube, usually made out of wood, that is hollowed out and pebbles are placed inside

ranch and ranching supplies, *n. pl.* Equipment needed to maintain cattle and/ or horses on a ranch. Examples include: feed, branding irons, horseshoes, corrals, fresh water, and saddles.

range, *n.* Measurement of distance typically used to describe how far spaceships fly. A short-range vessel can fly within a specific system of planets, while a ship with a long range can travel anywhere in the 'Verse. In addition to manufacturing specifications, range may also be limited by the amount of fuel, supplies, and personnel a ship can carry.

rat, *v. sl.* Go to a law enforcement official or Alliance agent and turn over information pertaining to a known criminal or fugitive.

Reader, *n.* Colloquial term to describe a person who displays psychic abilities. First mentioned in "Out of Gas", when River is being discussed.

Reaver territory, *pr.n.* Reavers are concentrated in the Blue Sun System, but they occasionally raid the Georgia System and are spotted elsewhere in the black. They have never been seen in the Core.

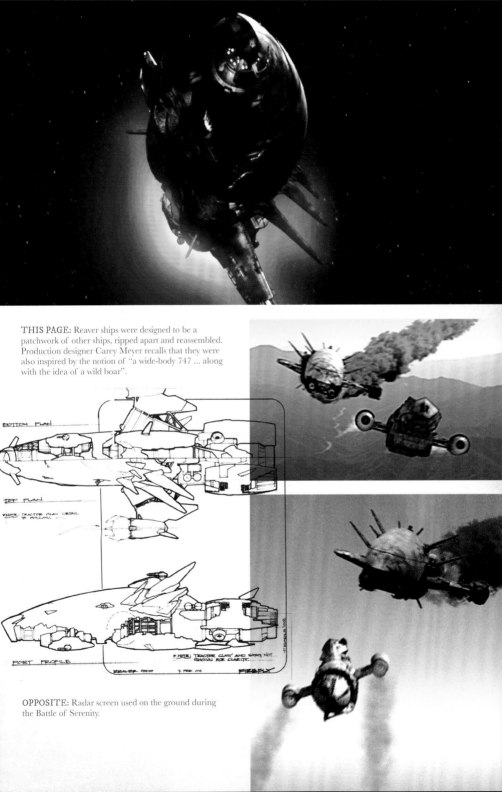

THIS PAGE: Reaver ships were designed to be a patchwork of other ships, ripped apart and reassembled. Production designer Carey Meyer recalls that they were also inspired by the notion of "a wide-body 747 ... along with the idea of a wild boar".

BOTTOM PLAN

TOP PLAN

NOTE: TRACTOR CLAW DETAIL TO FOLLOW.

PORT PROFILE

*NOTE: 'TRACTOR CLAW' AND WING NOT SHOWN FOR CLARITY.

REAVER SHIP   7 FEB 02   FIREFLY

OPPOSITE: Radar screen used on the ground during the Battle of Serenity.

Reavers, *n. pl. masc.* Men thought to have lost their sanity in the black. Once they go from human to savage, they cannot be saved. Reavers tend to fly in packs and operate ships that do not have core containment. They are mindless, merciless monsters bent on destruction. Typically, they target an area, leave a victim behind in a proto-Reaver state, and then return to claim that territory as their own. Most citizens who live in the Central planets do not believe Reavers exist, and think they're a story made up to frighten children and travelers from veering too far into space.

ZOË: You've never heard of Reavers?

SIMON: Campfire stories ... Men gone savage at the edge of space, killing and ...

ZOË: They're not stories.

SIMON: What happens if they board us?

ZOË: If they take the ship, they'll rape us to death, eat our flesh and sew our skins into their clothing ... and if we're very, very lucky, they'll do it in that order.

—"Serenity"

Red Sun System, *pr.n.* Planets that make up part of the Border. Examples include: Jiangyin, Greenleaf, and St Albans.

reg couple or **reg-couple,** *n.* Attachment that connects two ship parts, located in the rear of the ship.

Regina, *pr.n.* Planet located in the Georgia System. Featured in "The Train Job".

Renshaw, *pr.n.* Fellow smuggler. Desperate to hire Wash, but Mal beat him to it. Mentioned in "Out of Gas".

reputation, *n.* Views of other people regarding a person or larger entity, like the Blue Sun Corporation. Adelai Niska is obsessed with the concept of reputation and acts accordingly. He holds other people accountable to the terms of his deals in order to preserve his all-important reputation, without exception. This was a driving factor that eventually led to the events that took place in "War Stories".

retinal scan, *n.* Method to verify identification using biometrics on a subject's eye. The results are more authoritative and foolproof than any data or reports gleaned from scanning an ident card.

retrofit, *v.* Modify a component or system to add a new part or function that was not intended when it was first invented.

reverse-ambush, *n.* A synonym for surprise attack. Often used in combat.

reward, *n.* Payment for an item, information, or person. May be publicly broadcast to attract interest. The reward for River's capture was 200,000 credits.

Reynolds, Malcolm, *pr.n.* Captain of *Serenity* and veteran of the Unification War. Held the rank of sergeant and fought for the Independents with Corporal Zoë Alleyne. Present at several key battles, including the

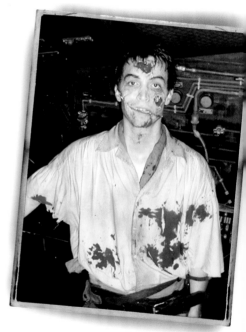

ABOVE: The survivor/killer from "Bushwhacked" looking the part of a proto-Reaver in full blood and gore.

Malcolm Reynolds

alcolm Reynolds' dialogue is an amalgamation of his life growing up on the Border planets and the time he served in the Unification War. As a military veteran, words and phrases sometimes slip into his vocabulary that relate to his experiences as a sergeant. He is also an emotional character and his speech reflects his feelings. When he's being sarcastic or taunting an opponent, he'll throw out a memorable line like: "I swear by my pretty floral bonnet I will end you." Often, Mal will drop the "g" from a word ending in -ing like other characters who hail from the Border or rim, but won't do so every time. To talk like Mal, pay attention to how the writers choose specific words that ebb and flow along with his terrible luck. Captain Reynolds is also memorable for having a lot of lines, usually swear words or interjections, spoken in Mandarin Chinese.

"It never goes smooth. How come it never goes smooth?" –"Safe"

In the "Serenity" teleplay, Mal's original line in Chinese was "Fuck everyone in the universe to death", but it didn't make it into the final cut. Was that changed?

Whedon: Yes. Probably changed. But we did have "the explosive diarrhea of an elephant", which is apparently more acceptable.

Mal-speak:

"We just gotta keep our heads down and do the job. Pray there ain't no more surprises."

"It's a simple job. And we're simple folk, so it shouldn't be a problem."

"I laid the fellow out. Seems to me the transaction is complete. Also satisfying."

"Ah, the pitter patter of tiny feet in combat boots."

"This is not my best day ever."

"We're down to the wire on fuel cells. We run hot, we might not even make it". – Wash, "Serenity"

war-ending Battle of Serenity, and is one of the few survivors from his unit. Like many Browncoats, Malcolm Reynolds refused to live under the rule of the Alliance, so he purchased a ship that allows him to fly free for as long as he can.

rim, the, *n.* Area of space furthest from the Central planets. The Blue Sun and Kalidasa Systems are both considered to be part of the rim. This area tends to hold less Alliance interest than the Core or Border planets, because it's the newest area of the 'Verse and the least civilized. While the Alliance does encourage settlers to start a new life out on the rim, this section of the 'Verse is plagued with Reavers, mercenaries, petty criminals, and shady opportunists like Rance Burgess

who strike backroom deals with Alliance representatives to keep the peace.

rounds, *n. pl.* Unit of measurement that describes the quantity of ammunition in a weapon. One round is equal to one piece of ammunition, like a bullet.

Ruby, *pr.n.* Little girl suffering from post-traumatic stress who didn't speak. River understood what had happened to her by reading her thoughts in "Safe" on Jiangyin.

ruckus, *n.* Fight. Argument. Could refer to a verbal conflict or a physical one.

rudderless, *adj. sl.* Directionless. Making decisions aimlessly. Going through the motions.

run hot, *id.* Flying a ship at great speeds, which burns more fuel.

rut, *v. vul.* To have sex like an animal.

S.S. Walden, *pr.n.* Name of the legal salvage ship that responded to *Serenity*'s distress call in "Out of Gas". Her captain was flanked by four crewmembers: Marco, Billy, Jesse, and Stern.

Sabbath, *pr.n.* Day of rest, according to the Bible.

Saffron, *pr.n.* Serial con artist and former Companion who appeared in "Our Mrs Reynolds" and "Trash". The only fact that's really known about her is that she never tells the truth.

"Sailor's Wife, The", *pr.n.* Ancient, traditional song from Earth-That-Was that originated in Ireland. Called a "jig". There

are multiple arrangements of this song. River Tam danced to one prior to Simon's kidnapping in "Safe".

sake, *n.* Traditional Japanese rice wine. There are many varieties and flavors.

salvage, *n.* Ship wreckage that may include supplies. In order to salvage ships, interested parties must file a permit to get permission from the government to retrieve cargo. The *Serenity* crew collects, sells, and trades salvage, but their work is considered a crime because they have

BELOW: Kaylee rummages through salvage for parts at an Ariel City municipal junkyard in "Ariel".

ABOVE: *Serenity* flying above a planet's atmosphere. Her captain, Mal, named the ship after the Battle of Serenity.
OPPOSITE: Example of Alliance propaganda. This poster invites citizens to visit Serenity Valley, the "birthplace of unity", on Hera. Poster designed by QMx.

not properly registered their ship and personnel to do so. Illegal salvagers are commonly found throughout the 'Verse, and many are veterans of the Unification War who fought for the Independents, like comrades Mal and Zoë.

sanguine, *adj.* 1. Upbeat and positive regardless of the circumstances. Optimistic in emergency situations. *n.* 2. Crimson. The color of blood.

Santo, *pr.n.* Planet in the White Sun System. Location of the opening scene in "Shindig".

Sclevages, Beauma, R.N., *pr.n.* Name printed on Wash's E.M.T. badge in "Ariel".

second, *n.* Swordsman ready to replace the main fighter in a duel if that person cannot make it.

secondary, *adj.* Backup. Most ship's systems are engineered to be redundant, i.e. to have a secondary, duplicated system that can be accessed or activated in the event of an emergency.

security sub-station, *n.* Secret broadcast channel law enforcement officials and agents use to communicate with one another.

septic system, *n.* Equipment designed to facilitate the collection and sanitary disposal of human waste. Ships built to fly longer distances and transport multiple passengers are equipped with a primary septic system. Larger ships may have auxiliary or tertiary systems. Typically smaller ships, like a one- or two-man fighter or a shuttle, do not have a standalone septic system.

septic tank, *n.* Container connected to a toilet that collects human waste. Part of the septic vac system.

septic vac, *n.* Vacuum used to empty a septic tank and dispose of human waste. Commonly found and used on ships.

Serenity, *pr.n.* Name of the Firefly-class ship owned by Captain Malcolm Reynolds. Its pilot is Hoban Washburne, and its mechanic is Kaylee Frye.

Serenity Valley, *pr.n.* Location of the infamous Battle of Serenity fought on Hera.

VISIT HISTORIC

SERENITY VALLEY

NATIONAL PARK

BIRTHPLACE OF UNITY

Inara Serra

Inara Serra is a Registered Companion who grew up in the Central planets. Her dialogue and bearing reflect a life of training and education at House Madrassa on Sihnon. A supporter of Unification, a Buddhist, and a member of the social elite, Inara speaks similarly to Simon Tam and uses proper grammar most of the time. While she tends to keep her emotions in check as part of her training, Inara does express her feelings through her conversations, for example with Kaylee. Often, the barbs she exchanges with Mal are sarcastic but not vulgar and, like Simon and Book, the Companion prides herself on her avoidance of curse words because she feels it's uncivilized.

Inara's use of Chinese is broader than the other characters in the show, but not as frequent. While the Companion does curse, primarily when speaking to Nandi in "Heart of Gold", she'll do so only on rare occasions.

"Every well-bred petty crook knows that the small, concealable weapons always go to the far left of the place setting." –"Heart of Gold"

Inara-speak:

"The time went too quickly."

"Is the petty criminal perchance ashamed to be riding with a Companion?"

"I don't suppose you'd find it up to the standards of your outings."

"In this company, Captain, I believe you are the one who stands out."

"What were you in the war? That big war you failed to win – you were a sergeant? Yeah, Sergeant Malcolm Reynolds, Balls and Bayonet Brigade, big tough veteran, now you got yourself a ship and you're a captain! Only I think you're still a sergeant, see. Still a soldier, man of honor in a den of thieves." – Badger, "Serenity"

ABOVE: Sergeant Malcolm Reynolds in action.

sergeant, *n.* 1. Military rank. Used by the Independent Faction in the Unification War. The person in command of a unit or platoon. *pr.n. uc.* 2. Title referring to rank held, i.e. Sergeant Malcolm Reynolds.

Serra, Inara, *pr.n.* Registered Companion and practicing Buddhist who grew up on Sihnon. Pays Mal a monthly stipend to rent a shuttle in order to conduct her business aboard *Serenity*. The story of how she came to be on board is revealed in "Out of Gas".

settlers, *n. pl.* People who stake a claim in the Border planets or rim with the intention of building a community. Unlike colonists, settlers are not necessarily acting in the interests of the Alliance, and may occupy a territory for a broad number of reasons ranging from the freedom to practice religious beliefs to the excitement of trying something new.

Shadow, *pr.n.* Planet located at the fringes of the Georgia System. Malcolm Reynolds grew up on a ranch located on this planet.

sharpshooter, *n.* Sniper. Person skilled with a rifle who hits their mark or near-impossible marks on a consistent basis.

Shepherd or **Shepard,** *pr.n.* Title for a religious official who's authorized to practice sacraments, like last rites, for believers of the faith. A Shepherd is a Christian who often wears a collar to denote his position and carries a Bible. They may serve their flocks in a variety of ways. Some become missionaries or remain in an abbey while others, like Shepherd Book, travel to seek God and help wherever needed.

MAL: Well, what about you, Shepherd? How come you're flying about with us brigands? I mean, shouldn't you be off bringing religiosity to the fuzzy-wuzzies or some such?
BOOK: Oh, I got heathens aplenty right here.
MAL: If I'm your mission, Shepherd, best give it up. You're welcome on my boat. God ain't.
– "The Train Job"

shimmerwine, *n.* Type of wine, like champagne, that shimmers beneath the light. Served at the dance during "Shindig".

shiny, *interj.* A.O.K. Most excellent. Everything's fine and dandy. Kaylee's favorite word.

Credit: Rocco Passionino (above left and right)

ABOVE: Exterior and interior of the *Serenity* shuttle rented by Inara.

"Sihnon isn't that different from this planet. More crowded, obviously, and I guess more complicated. The great city itself is … pictures can't capture it. It's like an ocean of light."

— Inara Serra, "Serenity"

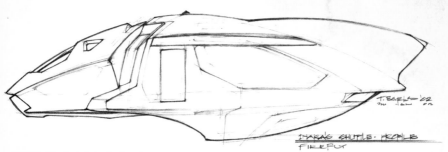

ABOVE: Tim Earls design for Inara's shuttle, one of two on *Serenity*.

Credit: Tim Earls

ship's papers, *n. pl.* Ship registration that is recorded on the Cortex. Accessible by law enforcement. Records the ship's history, identification, and the captain's name.

ship's seal, *n.* Mark approving the ship's papers as complete. The ship's seal has to be renewed annually. *Serenity*'s seal was found to be out-of-date in "Bushwhacked".

shoot-out, *n.* Gunfight involving a large number of people who are all firing at one another, i.e. the fight involving the Grange Brothers on Jiangyin.

shrapnel, *n.* Harmful remains of a bomb or incendiary device after it has detonated.

shuttle, *n.* Aircraft built to fly short distances. *Serenity* has two shuttles, one of which is occupied by Inara Serra.

sickhouse, *n. sl.* Makeshift hospital or unofficial building, usually a doctor's residence, that contains patients needing medical attention. Found on the Border

planets, like Jiangyin in "Safe", and the rim where credits and skilled personnel are in short supply.

Sihnon, *pr.n.* One of two capital planets in the Core. Inara Serra's home planet, and where she studied to be a Companion. She once remarked that Sihnon is similar to Persephone in appearance.

Silverhold colonies, *pr.n. pl.* Government-sanctioned colonies located in the Blue Sun System. Referenced in "The Message". Lieutenant Womack's official jurisdiction is for those colonies. His pursuit of Tracey Smith to St Albans was under the radar and his shady intentions were revealed by Shepherd Book.

single-person fighter, *n.* Small, short-range spacecraft manned by a single pilot. Also referred to as a "skiff".

skedaddle, *v. sl.* Scoot. Scurry quickly. Get out fast, e.g. "Let's skedaddle 'fore them feds show up!"

skunk, *n. sl.* Dirty rotten scoundrel. A bad-smelling backstabber or double-crosser. Used as an insult.

Skyplex, *pr.n.* Space station owned by Adelai Niska that is in orbit over the planet Ezra. The Skyplex is outfitted with a torture chamber, office, living quarters, several docks, etc. Niska's office, in particular, is an ostentatious display of his wealth. Like Atherton Wing, he also collects Earth-That-Was artifacts like the Tiffany lamp on

BELOW: *Serenity*'s official papers, bearing Mal's name. In "Safe", the Captain provides a false set of paperwork to avoid being scrutinized by the authorities.

ABOVE: The Alliance sonic rifle. Both Joss Whedon and the producers liked the idea of having a non-lethal weapon in the show, and it is used to this effect in "Ariel".

after the war. He fell in with the wrong crowd and attempted to outrun Lieutenant Womack in "The Message". Now deceased.

smoke canister, *n.* Chemical-based weapon favored by smugglers. Used in warfare to create artificial smoke in order to create a distraction. The smoke may be harmful or benign. Appeared in "The Train Job".

sniff the air, *id.* 1. Show disapproval or contempt for a specific location. The air isn't good enough to take a deep, restorative breath. *id.* 2. Find out information or listen to common gossip.

sonic rifle, *n.* Weapon employing sonar technology to harm or disable a target. A sonic rifle doesn't have any bullets, and is used by the Alliance in place of a stun gun. The sonic rifle appeared in "Ariel".

soup-catcher, *n. masc. sl.* Wild and unruly beard, moustache, or handlebar moustache. The hair is so out-of-control it prevents spills.

sourcebox, *n.* Device, like a modem, that allows the user to access the Cortex. Sourceboxes come in all shapes and sizes, and may also be operated for personal use, e.g. "a dedicated sourcebox".

Southdown Abbey, *pr.n.* Abbey located on Persephone in the White Sun System near Eavesdown Docks. Shepherd Book is from Southdown Abbey, and paid for his passage on *Serenity* with fresh produce and spices he brought from his home.

souvenir dish, *n.* Plate, bowl, or cup painted with a design commemorating that location. The Oriental souvenir dish Kaylee admired in "Safe" was titled "Prairie Paradise".

space station, *n.* Class of vessel that other ships can dock with. Tends to remain in a stationary orbit due to its size and so it can be easily found. Niska's Skyplex and Li Shen's Space Bazaar are both space stations.

spacesuit, *n.* Specialized suit that allows a

his desk. Shown in "The Train Job" and "War Stories."

slave trade, *n.* Illegal kidnapping of human beings with the intention of selling them like commodities to interested parties. The slave trade provides cheap labor and is active outside the Central planets. A chained line of slaves were shown standing in Badger's office in "Serenity".

Smith, Tracey, *pr.n.* Former Independent private who made all the wrong decisions

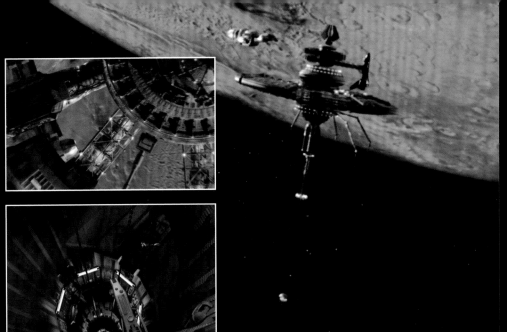

BELOW: The spacesuits worn in *Firefly* were originally designed for the Kurt Russell movie *Soldier*.

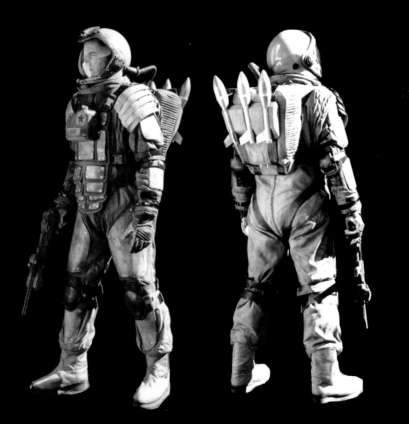

STAFF
ST. LUCY'S MEDICAL CENTER
强健
Beauma Sclevages R.N.
013 548
DEPARTMENT
72382 3575873

STAFF
ST. LUCY'S MEDICAL CENTER
强健
Kiki LaRue R.N.
013 548
DEPARTMENT
72382 3575873

STAFF
ST. LUCY'S MEDICAL CENTER
强健
Q. Kumamota RN
013 548
DEPARTMENT
72382 3575873

STAFF
ST. LUCY'S MEDICAL CENTER
强健
Miles Arixoen M.D.
013 548
DEPARTMENT
72382 3575873

THIS PAGE: The *Serenity* crew's forged staff passes and various images showing different parts of St Lucy's Medical Center. Hospitals like this one fall under the purview of the Alliance, and often have an office set up for their use (as seen below).

human being to temporarily survive in space. Spacesuits were used by Simon and River Tam when they were hiding from the Alliance in "Bushwhacked".

spaceworthy, *n.* Ship that is capable of travelling successfully through space, without falling apart or suffering from some other mechanical malfunction.

speech, *n.* Spoken word. In the 'Verse, citizens who grow up in the Central planets have more access to education and their formal way of speaking tends to reflect their years of study. For this reason, Border-planet and rim natives are often typecast as backwards because their level of education is either poor or they have the tendency to speak colloquially, using slang words, idiomatic phrases, and an adopted meaning of a word. While the colloquial speakers and the "proper" language users can understand one another, a number of judgments and stereotypes result based on their exchanges. People who live in the Core are seen as wealthy, confident, and carefree because they have everything they could possibly want. People who live everywhere else are considered less valuable because they're poor, in dire straits, or are criminals. In many ways, the language usage of the 'Verse is a display of the age-old class struggle between rich and poor.

spices, *n. pl.* Herbs, salt, and other natural seasonings, like rosemary or marjoram, that make the taste of food more palatable. Fresh spices are commonly grown in gardens, like the one Shepherd Book maintained in Southdown Abbey, but are harder to come by in dry, arid climates. Spices are a valuable trading commodity.

St Albans, *pr.n.* Snowy planet located in the Red Sun System. Tracey Smith was buried here near his home in "The Message".

St Lucy's Medical Center, *pr.n.* Name of the hospital the *Serenity* crew targets in "Ariel". Though it is open to the public, it is a government-run facility.

starboard, *n.* 1. Direction used in flight and sailing, to turn to the right, e.g. "Check the starboard engine." *adj.* 2. Pertaining to the right side, or right-handed control or object, e.g. "the starboard exhaust".

Stark, *pr.n.* Kidnapper who snatched Simon Tam and took him and his sister back to the settlement on Jiangyin in "Safe".

steamer, *n.* Major engine part that consists of smaller parts, like the compression coil.

sticky, the, *n. sl.* Piece of equipment that applies a chemical adhesive. Part of the process the crew devised to break through the hull of a derelict.

strawberry, *n.* Fresh berry enjoyed by Kaylee in "Serenity". The fruit is rare and hard to come by for travelers.

Stuart, Jerome, *pr.n.* Friend of Gabriel Tam and the new Head of Surgery at AMI on Osiris. Referred to in "Safe".

sumbitch, *n. interj. vul. masc.* Or sommbitch, sonbitch. Literally, son of a bitch.

summat, *adv. sl.* Alternate form of somewhat.

surveyor, *n.* Professional who scouts out new territories in land, sea, or space and records the information. Surveyors are commonly found among colonists and settlers on the Border planets and rim.

synchronizers, *n. pl.* Mechanical parts used to help decrease irregularities in two ship systems or to help parts work in tandem. Kaylee found synchronizers in "Ariel" in the junkyard.

ABOVE: Kaylee enjoys a juicy strawberry in "Serenity".

River Tam

*They weren't cows inside.
They were waiting to be, but they
forgot. Now they see sky and
they remember what they are.*

— "Safe"

Rescued from the Academy by her brother, Simon, River spends most of her time recovering from her ordeal. Her dialogue points to her trauma as well as her rare moments of lucidity. When she's lucid, River shows remarkable insight and is able to quickly adapt in stressful situations. In "Shindig", she skilfully adopted a Cockney accent to speak to Badger. In "Out of Gas", she "comforts" Book by explaining how the crew would die in space in a matter-of-fact manner. When her mind isn't clear, however, her oddly worded dialogue hints at her psychic abilities. While the crew doesn't speculate on River's true nature as a Reader until "Objects in Space", the way she talks reveals volumes of information about her character for those who are willing to listen.

Erratic and unpredictable, River's only constant is her brother, Simon, and her speech is a clear sign of her fluctuating mental health. She can and does curse, but it's important to keep in mind that while she can divert to a more casual way of speaking, she was brought up in the Central planets. Her only line in Chinese as an adult is directed at Mal when she curses at him during "Safe".

River-speak:

"Sure, I got a secret. More'n one."

"This isn't home."

tachy, *n. abbr.* Short for tachycardia. State in which the heart beats irregularly. To "go tachy" means the heartbeat is abnormal.

Tall Card, *pr.n.* Type of poker played by *Serenity* crewmembers that allowed them to bid chores instead of credits.

Tam, Gabriel, *pr.n.* Simon and River's father who lives on Ariel. A member of high society and an Alliance loyalist. Simon remembered him in flashbacks that explore their relationship in "Safe".

Tam, Regan, *pr.n.* Simon and River Tam's mother.

Tam, River, *pr.n.* Alliance fugitive, rescued government experiment, and former gifted student with a bright future.

Tam, Simon, *pr.n.* Brilliant ship's doctor and River's devoted brother. During "Ariel", it is clear that he has become an Alliance fugitive as well. Over time, he developed feelings for Kaylee.

Tanaka, *pr.n.* Fellow smuggler. Gave Wash a great reference. Mentioned in "Out of Gas".

technobabble, *n.* Technology-based words and phrases that are not understood by laypeople. For example, Kaylee uses technical descriptions to describe problems

BELOW: Tall Card, aka Chore Poker, was originally designed to be played with these distressed metal cards.

Simon Tam

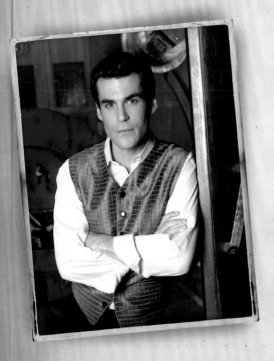

Simon Tam is a well-educated citizen whose manners and upbringing reflect an upper-class life in the Core. A former supporter of Unification, the doctor is well versed in medical jargon, which he uses often. Though Simon is often required to patch up bullet holes and stitch stab wounds, his medical vocabulary is a mixture of twenty-first- and twenty-sixth-century advances in healthcare that border on science fiction.

At the beginning of the show, Simon is often restrained and his words reflect his hesitancy to get to know the crew. Though he begins to open up as the episodes progress, the doctor reveals that his proper way of speaking is also cultural. In "Jaynestown", Simon tells Kaylee that: "My way of being polite or however, it's ... well, it's the only way I have of showing you that I like you. Of showing respect."

The doctor tries to refrain from cursing for the same reasons that Inara does, and tends to speak in complete sentences that are grammatically correct. Simon's lines in Chinese range from simple questions to the occasional curse word.

Simon-speak:

"Sorry if my criminal instincts aren't as sharp as the rest of your crew."

"This may come as a shock, but I'm actually not very good at talking to girls."

"I 'selflessly' turned us both into wanted fugitives."

"These phrases ... they don't sound like her."

"I'm always amazed at what she knows."

"I am very smart. I went to the best Medacad in Osiris, top three percent of my class, finished my internship in eight months. 'Gifted' is the term."

— "Jaynestown"

with or functions of a ship, and to Mal it sounds like technobabble.

temple, *n.* Place of worship where Buddhists go to practice their faith.

temporal lobe, *n.* Area of the brain concerned with language recall and the formation of new memories.

terraforming, *n.* Science of converting an inhabitable celestial body into a world that can sustain human life. In order for humanity to live in the 'Verse, terraforming equipment was used to convert dead planets into earth-like worlds. The process of terraforming a planet is highly complex and doesn't always work. In the Border, newly terraformed planets and moons may cause the contraction of a specific disease when the land is mined due to an adverse chemical reaction. Terraforming, which is overseen by the Alliance, did not transform the planet Regina properly and its miners contracted Bowden's Malady. In many cases, the Alliance will supply medicine to cure illnesses caused by terraforming to its citizens to alleviate their suffering and increase the yield of a mine, field, ranch, or factory. Due to the dangerous nature of the work, some terraformers utilize indentured servants or slaves to operate terraforming equipment.

thermal cap, *n.* Heat-and-fireproof covering for a ship part. Prevents a mechanic from being burned when it's touched.

thick, *adj.* Stupid or dense, e.g. "You're just too thick-headed to understand what I'm saying."

three-point watch, *n.* Military tactic involving three people tasked with looking out for enemy combatants.

torture board, *n.* Tall slats used to bind victims and prepare them for torture. Wash and Mal were attached to torture boards in "War Stories".

torture spider, *n.* Unique implement of torture devised by Adelai Niska. The device is attached to the flesh and the

ABOVE: A torture board was used by the Torturer in "War Stories" to inflict pain on Wash and Mal.

spider is activated by a machine. When in contact with the flesh, the torture spider emits electricity. Used in "War Stories".

Torturer, *pr.n.* Employee of Adelai Niska who specializes in inflicting pain. The

Torturer has perfected the art of killing his victims and then reviving them to suffer more pain. Appeared in "War Stories".

tour, *n.* Military term used to describe the route of a ship like an Alliance cruiser.

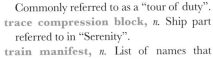

Commonly referred to as a "tour of duty".

trace compression block, *n.* Ship part referred to in "Serenity".

train manifest, *n.* List of names that records the passengers on any given train. Referred to in "The Train Job". Sheriff Bourne's review of the train manifest is what led to Mal and Zoë being questioned and almost revealed as criminals.

trajectory, *n.* Curve calculated by a mathematical formula used to predict a ship's flight path.

transport ship, *n.* Type of vessel engineered to fly goods and people from one location to another. Transport ships are not equipped with weapons.

Trans-U, *pr.n.* Older commercial vessel. Reavers flew this model of ship, without a core containment, in "Serenity".

tripwire, *n.* Component in a trap. A taut wire is strung between two points, usually on the ground. When a person walks or trips over the wire, the trap is activated.

Triumph, *pr.n.* Planet in the Red Sun System and home to the Triumph Settlers.

Triumph Settlers, *pr.n. pl.* The lifestyle of this group is similar to that of the Amish people from Earth-That-Was. Their leader, Elder Gommen, hired the *Serenity* crew to solve their troubles with local bandits in "Our Mrs Reynolds". Part of the payment was a wife for Mal. In their culture, according to Book: "Divorce is very rare and requires dispensation from her pastor".

BOOK: It says here, the woman lays the wreath upon her intended – which I do recall – which represents his sovereignty.

MAL: (to Saffron) That was you?

BOOK: And he drinks of her wine. This represents his obeisance to the life-giving blood of her – I'll skip this part – and then there's a dance, with a joining of hands. (Closes book.) The marriage ceremony of the Triumph Settlers, been so over eighty years. You, sir, are a newlywed.

– "Our Mrs Reynolds"

truss, *v.* To bind a person or object up tightly.

truthsome, *adj.* Truthful. Honest.

tweak, *v. sl.* Act like a person who has ingested too many illicit drugs. May be used literally or figuratively.

twenty-sixth century, *n.* Futuristic time period corresponding to the events in the TV show. *Firefly* begins in the year 2517.

Two-Fry, *pr.n.* Sharpshooter who worked for Patience on the moon Whitefall. Now deceased.

two-six-two, *n.* Name of an official communications channel. Its users can securely transmit and receive important messages.

RIGHT: When he consulted the train's manifest, Sheriff Bourne found Mal and Zoë's story of being newlyweds seeking mining work highly suspicious.

OPPOSITE: Adelai Niska's innovative 'torture spider' prop was printed into existence using a 3D wax printer.

BELOW: *Serenity* flies over the hovertrain to lower itself into position for the crew's heist.

Unification, *pr.n.* Philosophy that all planets and moons should fall under the purview of a single governing body, as opposed to allowing them to operate independently of one another. The concept of Unification is what led to the Unification War according to Alliance propaganda. Most Alliance loyalists and Central-planet citizens supported Unification, while the rest of the 'Verse did not.

Unification Day or **U-Day,** *pr.n.* Annual holiday commemorating the end of the Unification War. The day the Independent Faction forces laid down their arms and surrendered to the Alliance on Hera.

Unification War, *pr.n.* Major conflict fought between the Alliance, who governed the resource- and population-rich Central planets, and the Independent Faction for the right to rule. The Alliance used all of the resources at its disposal to promote Unification as a beneficial concept. It fought in the name of Unification and convinced its populace that the military was just and righteous. The government also claimed the Independent Faction were rebels that threatened to harm the stability of the Central planets. The Independents, on the other hand, struggled for the right to keep the Alliance

at bay and to allow planetary and lunar citizens to decide for themselves who their leaders were. They believed the Alliance was acting like a fascist dictator, a feeling that has since been proven true. At first, the two sides had a number of discussions, but these key philosophical differences could not be resolved in peace talks. Eventually, this led to many battles fought throughout the Central planets like the Battle of Du-Khang and the war-ending Battle of Serenity. Eventually, the Independent Faction negotiated terms of surrender, and the Alliance pursued and destroyed Independent ships and munitions.

Union of Allied Planets, *pr.n.* Official title that refers to the territories the government oversees. Every planet and moon in the 'Verse is a member of the Union of Allied Planets which are, in turn, governed by the Anglo-Sino Alliance.

Universal Alliance, *pr.n.* Alternate name for the Anglo-Sino Alliance.

Universal Encyclopedia, *pr.n.* 1. Body of work containing audio-visual reference material collecting human knowledge in various fields of study like anthropology, history, and geography. The data, which can be contained on a datastick, is government-approved and contains Alliance propaganda, e.g. the Unification War is relayed from the government's perspective, and turns the Independent Faction into villains. *pr.n.* 2. Case containing multiple datasticks. User places a datastick in the case's spine to access, display, and listen to data on a small touch screen.

ABOVE: This Universal Encyclopedia filled with datasticks is owned by Simon Tam. Its design was based on a Franklin personal organizer.

OPPOSITE: Fighting during the Unification War.

vasoconstriction, *n.* Narrowing of the body's blood vessels. Occurs when small muscles in vessels contract, which reduces or blocks blood flow. The vessels' constriction may be caused by a number of factors ranging from changes in temperature to various medicines or psychological states.

vasoconstrictor, *n.* Category of medicine given to patients to help regulate blood pressure. Often given to patients suffering from acute blood loss either from a wound or during surgery. Alprazaline push is a type of vasoconstrictor.

vasodilation, *n.* Widening of the body's blood vessels. Dilation occurs when the vessels' small muscles relax, thereby increasing blood flow. Like vasoconstriction, this may result from a variety of causes.

vasodilator, *n.* Type of medicine administered to patients to increase blood flow to tissues or organs, to speed up the healing process. Adenosine is a type of vasodilator.

Vektor, *pr.n.* Manufacturer of a pistol used by Simon Tam.

Vera, *pr.n.* Pet name for a large rifle used by Jayne Cobb. The mercenary is emotionally attached to this gun, but is willing to make a deal with it for Saffron in "Our Mrs Reynolds".

'Verse, *pr.n.* 1. Area of settled space encompassing all systems containing celestial bodies where humans live. *n. lc. abbr.* 2. Short form for universe.

vidphone, *n.* Visual communications device used to call an individual over the Cortex. May be a public or private vidphone. Public vidphones are mounted into a wall or façade and can be found in most major cities in the Central planets. Jayne called the feds using a public vidphone in "Ariel".

Viktor, *pr.n.* Adelai Niska's assistant. His whereabouts following the conclusion of "War Stories" are unknown. He may have died in the shoot-out.

Vitelli, *pr.n.* Independent officer who deserted his post during the Battle of Du-Khang.

LEFT: Jayne's beloved Vera was adapted for the show by Gibbons Ltd from a weapon used in the Robert de Niro movie *Showtime*.

VERA'S VITALS

LENGTH: 90 cm

HEIGHT, top of scope to bottom of mag: 45 cm

WIDTH: 7 cm at widest point

CAPACITY: 12 rounds

CALIBER: 12 gauge

CONSTRUCTION: CNC machined aluminum alloy components anodized in lilac, blue, and gold. Some steel parts and phenolic-impregnated, laminated wood grips

WEIGHT: Around 12.69 kg (28 lbs)

RIGHT: Jayne's gun cleaning kit and backup pistol. The kit allows him to ensure Vera and his other arms are well maintained.

OPPOSITE: Simon's Vektor stunt pistol.

Hoban "Wash" Washburne

WASH (Steg): Curse your sudden
but inevitable betrayal!
WASH (T-rex): Ha HA! Mine is
an evil laugh! Now die!
– "Serenity"

from the Border, rim, or Central planets. He doesn't speak "properly" like Inara, Simon, or Shepherd Book, but he doesn't heavily rely on slang such as "good'n" or "flyin'" to get his point across either. Wash does use some contractions, like "'cause" or "'stead", but typically won't truncate his sentences. The pilot tends to speak clearly and can talk in technobabble with Kaylee just as easily as he can about his marriage to Zoë.

Unlike his wife, Wash will chatter away (or stutter) nervously and holds nothing back. Mal used this knowledge to keep Wash alive in "War Stories" by ensuring he kept talking and stayed angry. Apropos of his character, Wash swears in Chinese to convey moments of surprise or, when he's butting heads with Mal like he did in "Out of Gas", anger or dismay.

*S*erenity's pilot, Wash, has a unique way of speaking that is reflected whenever the character is a little nervous about what's going to happen next. Wash doesn't use dialogue befitting a character who hails

---

Wash-speak:

"Well there goes Plan A..."

"We gotta go to the crappy town where I'm a hero ..."

"I vote we do this job really really fast."

"He's dampening my team spirit."

"Get you close enough to ring the doorbell."

W

Washburne, Hoban "Wash", *pr.n.* Top-notch pilot who flies *Serenity*. Married to Zoë.

Washburne, Zoë Alleyne, *pr.n.* Former Corporal in the Unification War who fought for the Independents. She is first mate on board *Serenity* and Wash's wife.

washing of feet, *n.* 1. Christian religious rite performed on Earth-That-Was. *v.* 2. Act that mimics the Good Shepherd's deed in the Bible. In "Our Mrs Reynolds", when Saffron offers to wash Mal's feet, she is pretending to be unworthy of and subordinate to her husband.

wave, *n.* Private, audio-visual message transmitted over the Cortex. May be a recorded message or occur in real time. Signal strength and image clarity depends upon the level of technology used to access the message over the Cortex. Waves may also be scrambled, encrypted, or intercepted.

weak tea, *id.* Not strong enough or did not pay well.

"Last two jobs we had were weak tea. We got nothing saved, and taking on passengers won't help near enough."
– Mal, "Serenity"

weave, *n.* Hypoallergenic, synthetic bandage used by medical personnel to cover wounds on the body. Common medical device found in every medkit, infirmary, and hospital.

wetware, *n.* 1. Illegally produced bio-engineered organs and tissue that are sold as a commodity in the criminal

BELOW: Zoë shows her appreciation for husband Wash after his ordeal at the hands of Niska in "War Stories".

Zoë Alleyne Washburne

A former corporal in the Unification War and *Serenity*'s first mate, Zoë Alleyne Washburne speaks similarly to the Captain – if and when she chooses to do so. The strength of Zoë's dialogue isn't always found in what she says, it's what she doesn't say that's often telling about her character. When she's pressed by Commander Harken to talk about her marriage in "Bushwhacked", for example, Zoë isn't willing to share that information with the feds. Though she found a way to put the Unification War behind her by marrying Wash, Zoë still refers to Mal as "Sir". She is also not afraid to make a cutting remark when the situation calls for it, like she often does when putting Jayne Cobb in his place.

Like Mal and Kaylee, Zoë's dialogue does incorporate slang words such as "slink" and alternate spellings of words like "wanna".

To talk like Zoë, keep in mind that, even when she's swearing, Zoë's dialogue shows she's not prone to emotional outbursts. Her lines typically range from simple warnings to the occasional interjection.

Zoë-speak:

"Hold this position. We lose this ground, we lose it all."

"First rule of battle, little one. Never let 'em know where you are."

underground. A blastomere is considered wetware. *n.* 2. Organic material designed to replicate the functions of, or behave similarly to, a computer system. *n.* 3. Brain that acts like a computer hard drive.

wetwire, *v. sl.* Opposite of hardwire. Instead of permanently attaching wires to an interface, console, or part, wires are temporarily connected to repair a ship's system or temporarily create a desired effect.

whiskers, *n. pl. masc.* Hair growing on a man's face.

White Sun System, *pr.n.* The seat of the Alliance's power and civilization. Also referred to as the Core and the Central planets. Bellerophon, Persephone, Ariel, and Osiris are examples of planets found in this system.

Whitefall, *pr.n.* Fourth moon of the planet Athens in the Georgia System. The crew flew to Whitefall to meet Patience in "Serenity".

whore, *n. fem.* Women or men who trade sexual favors for money. Prostitutes are considered undesirable by civilized society, and are typically female. In the Central planets, a sex worker may be arrested for pretending to be a Companion or turned over to the Guild for punishment and evaluation.

whorehouse, *n. fem.* Brothel where sex workers ply their trade. Like prostitutes, whorehouses are not sanctioned by the Guild. Thus, they are illegal and may be shut down by law enforcement, which is why they tend to operate outside of the Core. The Heart of Gold is the name of a whorehouse on Deadwood in the Blue Sun System.

BELOW: The *Serenity* crew met with Patience on Whitefall in the Georgia System.

RIGHT: Foil was used to give the Heart of Gold whorehouse a sci-fi feel but the effect was such that Joss Whedon affectionately referred to it as "the Jiffy-Pop mansion".

ABOVE: Inara arranged to meet client Atherton Wing in "Shindig", but his intentions proved to be dishonorable.

ABOVE: Wright playing a game of holopool on Santo with Mal and Jayne.

Wing, Atherton, *pr.n.* Socialite who asks Inara to become his personal Companion. Accepts a challenge to a duel by Mal, and his actions earn him a black mark in the client registry during "Shindig".

witch, *n. fem.* According to the Bible, an evil female who is in league with the Devil and granted magical powers. River is accused of being a witch in "Safe" after displaying her psychic abilities.

SIMON: What's wrong?

DORALEE: "And they shall be among the people, and they shall speak truths and whisper secrets ... and you will know them by their crafts ..."

SIMON: What are you talking about?

DORALEE: "Thou shall not suffer a witch to live."

– "Safe"

Witchcraft, *n.* Biblical reference to dark arts performed by agents of the Devil. Belief in the supernatural is more common in outlying or isolated settlements, like the shantytown on Jiangyin, and is an amalgamated distortion of cultural, religious, or philosophical ideologies and beliefs that originated on Earth-That-Was.

Womack, Lieutenant, *pr.n.* Corrupt Alliance law enforcement official in pursuit of Tracey Smith during "The Message".

woman, *n. fem.* Human female.

World Council, *pr.n.* Governing body of a planet and its moons. In "War Stories", the World Council, which oversees the planet Ezra and its moons in the Georgia System, has been corrupted by Adelai Niska. The World Council's jurisdiction ends at the planetary boundary.

wrassle, *v. sl.* 1. Wrestle playfully with a friend or love interest. *v. sl.* 2. Get into a fight with an opponent, human or animal, e.g. "Is it true you wrassle snakes?"

Wright, *pr.n.* Slaver who kidnaps people and sells them to Allied terraforming crews stationed in the Border planets. Wright and his partner, Holder, play holopool with Mal and Jayne on Santo, until Mal's code gets the better of him. After the Captain steals the slaver's cash, a bar fight ensues in "Shindig".

OPPOSITE: Few facts are known about Yo-Saf-Bridge, and her true identity.

X Y Z

yammer, *v.* 1. Talk loudly and often. *v.* 2. Complain or whine frequently, and in an annoying fashion.

yokel, *n. sl.* Country bumpkin. Bumbling peasant. Illiterate and without manners. Meant as an insult.

Yolanda, *pr.n.* Alias used by Saffron in "Trash". Yolanda was married to Durran Haymer and lived on Bellerophon. She returned home with Mal to steal her ex-husband's prized possession.

Yo-Saf-Bridge, *pr.n. abbr. sl.* Yo-Saf-Bridge stands for a trio of aliases. Yolanda Saffron Bridget. Yo-Saf-Bridge is Mal's nickname for the con artist and former Companion who almost got him killed.

Yu, Shan, *pr.n.* Historical Chinese personage, possibly from Earth-That-Was. Shan Yu was, according to Shepherd Book and Simon Tam, a psychotic dictator and warrior poet who wrote many books about war and torture. Shan Yu is also Adelai Niska's inspiration. Many references to Yu can be found in "War Stories".

"He said, 'Live with a man forty years, share his house, his meals, speak on every subject. Then tie him up and hold him over the volcano's edge. And on that day you will finally meet the man.'"

– Shepherd Book quoting Shan Yu, "War Stories"

Zelle, *pr.n.* Socialite and friend of Banning Miller in "Shindig".

zero grav, *n. abbr.* Short for zero gravity. State of weightlessness caused by the lack of gravitational forces. Most, if not all, twenty-sixth-century spaceships have a primary and auxiliary system that generates artificial gravity. Airlocks are also engineered to create artificial gravity in situations where one ship is connected to another.

For the Love of Pinyin

An interview with *Firefly* Chinese translator Jenny Lynn

Tell us a little bit about yourself and your background.

I was born and raised in Southern California by parents who emigrated to the U.S. from Taiwan. So, full disclosure, I'm far from being an expert in Chinese since I learned Taiwanese, Mandarin, and a little bit of Cantonese at home with my family and by attending Chinese School every Saturday. My parents used to have to drag me to Chinese School kicking and screaming, because who wants to go to school on a Saturday? But years later when this opportunity to help translate on *Firefly* came up, they were like, "See? Aren't you glad we made you stick with it?" Of course, nothing I learned in school would prepare me for the kind of language I had to translate on the show!

What makes Chinese so fascinating to study? What are the language's unique characteristics?

I suppose what makes it fascinating depends on the individual. I could go on all day about what I find fascinating about it. For one, it's really, really challenging. I grew up speaking it, did a refresher course in college, and still don't feel like I have a true handle on it.

One of the difficult things for me about Chinese is the written language, which consists of ideograms – characters and symbols that often represent the actual meaning of the word pictorially. For every word there is a different character that represents it. So think about all the words you know in your vocabulary and that's about as many characters as you need to memorize.

They've made things easier for Westerners

ABOUT JENNY LYNN:
A native of Southern California, Jenny graduated from Duke University with a degree in English. She's currently a TV writer-producer having worked on series for ABC, Fox, CW, and WeTV.

to learn Chinese with a "Romanized" system called "Pinyin". That is, they've come up with a system using our Roman or Latin alphabet to spell the words out. In my opinion, it's still not the most intuitive, like "x's" are pronounced "sh" and "q's" are pronounced "ch", but if you learn it you'll get the hang of it.

Anyway, if I haven't bored you already, that's just the reading and writing part of the equation.

Speaking Mandarin Chinese has a whole other set of challenges. It's a tonal language with four different tones (plus a fifth shortened staccato one used from time to time). So a word pronounced "ma" can mean "mother" or "measles" or "horse" or "anger" or even turn a whole sentence into a question depending on your voice inflection. It's probably the hardest part to nail down for non-native speakers. I think the trick is to think of it like music. And here's an interesting bit of trivia: apparently, there's a greater percentage of native Chinese speakers who have perfect musical pitch than any other population, they think because of the tonality we learn to distinguish at an early age.

Another unique quirk of Mandarin that's hard to learn is this weird rollback of the tongue that's like adding an "r" to some consonant clusters. It's particularly prominent in the Beijing dialect. So if you hear someone speak Mandarin and it sounds like they're about to swallow their tongue, they're most likely from Beijing.

Speaking of rollback, I'm pretty sure everybody's now rolled their eyes into their skull in boredom. *"Dude, can you just skip to the part where you teach me how to say 'asswipe'?"*

What was your position at Mutant Enemy?

Christopher Buchanan, who was the president of Mutant Enemy, hired me to be his creative executive. It was our job to manage Joss Whedon's empire while Joss was busy writing and running *Buffy the Vampire Slayer*, *Angel*, and *Firefly*. That meant everything from hiring writers for the shows to marketing and promoting the series. It was great, great fun to be involved in so much and to be around that level of talent. It's one of the best jobs I've ever had.

How did you come to work on *Firefly* as a translator?

Chris and I came to Mutant Enemy just as the pilot for *Firefly* was going into production. When I read the script, I was totally blown away by it and even giddier that there was going to be Chinese in it.

Someone had already translated the Chinese in the pilot into Mandarin pinyin. After the series got picked up, there was a day when our script coordinator, Neil Levin, was tearing his hair out trying to find a translator for the run of the show. I ran out of my office and was like, "Um, hello?" In his defense, he said he didn't want to be so presumptuous as to assume the Asian girl in the office next to him spoke Chinese. But that is the ever-so-scientific process of how that came to be.

Oh, and by the way, I only found out after the show was over that Joss actually wanted the Chinese to be Cantonese. I'd like to say for the record that the pilot was already done in Mandarin when I inherited the job. I just assumed I was supposed to continue where the other person had left off. But I still think using Mandarin over Cantonese makes sense given that Mandarin is the more prevalent form and the official standardized dialect in China and other Chinese-speaking countries.

Working on a TV show can be pretty demanding. Can you walk us through your role as translator?

As an exec for the company, I was always reading every draft that came in on all the shows. As the translator, I'd receive a printout from Neil of just the lines in the script that needed translating. Production requested that it be written out phonetically rather than in pinyin, since pinyin, as I mentioned, doesn't always look like how you'd pronounce it.

When it came to shooting time, I'd make audio cassette tapes (remember those?) for each actor and their lines for the episode – one time at conversational speed, three times slowly, then again at conversational speed, for every line. I also had to make another set of tapes for the on-set script supervisor, Jain Sekuler. She did her best to listen and make sure the actors were saying it right on the day, since it's the script supervisor's job to make sure everything in the script is shot in production. I wasn't able to be there on set to work with the actors or correct them because I had my regular job at Mutant Enemy to attend to. I wasn't on salary or contract to be the translator for the show; it was just this fun thing I got to do on the side.

Did you ever hear any complaints about the use of Chinese on *Firefly*?

I'd say the biggest gripe I hear about the Chinese on the show is how it sometimes got mutilated. It's really due to a combination of factors. One, I never got the opportunity to give the actors a primer on how to tackle it. Shooting a TV series is just go, go, go. They have so many things to worry about in addition to the couple of Chinese lines they have for an episode. Then, as I've said before, intonation for Mandarin is so important yet wicked hard to nail, even for those who've studied the language for years. For those who *do* understand Chinese, if the tone is even the slightest bit off then you're hearing something entirely different, possibly nonsensical. For instance, I was teaching a friend once how to ask someone in Chinese for their fax number. And she's like, "Fax number?" By merely raising her intonation as you do in English to ask a question, she wound up saying, "Is your fax machine doing well?" And, of course, the biggest factor, as I said before, was not being able to work with them on set. At least for the series. I got to do it on the movie.

What were some of the challenges you faced during the process of translating the lines into Mandarin?

Ha! I'm so glad you asked. Here were my challenges: I never learned to curse in Chinese because I learned from my folks and from Chinese School. So I have a very sanitized, goodie-two-shoes Chinese lexicon. That meant I actually had to call my mom for help on this show. I really have to give a big shout-out to her, because she's actually the unsung hero of the Chinese translations on *Firefly*.

The other big challenge was syntax. See, there's American English syntax, there's Mandarin Chinese syntax, and then there's Whedonese syntax – which, as fans know, is its own kind of awesome. So I got these lines where I could have found an easy equivalent to convey a general gist, but because they had their own genius of expression, I felt it behooved me to come up with something just as Whedonesque. That's why there were so many phone calls home to mom, me having learned a straightforward, school-taught form. It was really fun to put our heads together to muck up the grammar and get it just so. I've heard from a few Chinese speakers who thought some of the Chinese in *Firefly* was so odd. "You wouldn't say it like that." My response has always been, "If you only knew what it said in English." Which now they can in this lovely dictionary!

Earlier, you mentioned that the Chinese on the show was intended to be Cantonese. Which language do you feel is better to curse in?

You know … I've actually heard a few Cantonese priding themselves on being able to throw down a good verbal assault. Cantonese has harder-hitting consonants and some gnarly guttural, back-of-the-throat sounds. To me, it's like the German of Chinese dialects. So I suppose Joss had the right instinct to want Cantonese. *Gorramnit.* Sorry, Joss.

Oh, and here's a good example of how it comes across to the non-Chinese-trained ear. So on "Out of Gas," there's a part where the *Serenity* computer goes berserk because there's a life-support failure. The editor of the episode, Lisa Lassek, asked me one day to voice the audio track in Mandarin and English for an early cut of the episode. It was just a placeholder until a professional actor could be hired later to fill in the track. When they finally got the actor to do it, she did the line in Cantonese. I guess the producers had gotten used to hearing my voice and Mandarin is the more mellifluous dialect of the two, so they asked me if I'd be willing to join the Screen Actors Guild and be the voice of *Serenity* from there on out. Because, in their words, "That other woman sounded so mean." She didn't sound mean, she just sounded Cantonese!

Did you get to speak any other Chinese on the show?

Yes, after I joined the Screen Actors Guild I wound up voicing not only the *Serenity* computer, but also a few more background bits. I'd always secretly wanted to do voiceover work and I have to say, as fantasies go, it's a pretty great way to have one fulfilled. Plus, it's still fun to get a residual check now and then, if for nothing else than to know that the show's still playing somewhere on our planet.

What's your favorite *Firefly* line?

Wow, there are so many, especially those that come out of Jayne's mouth. But I'll say the most memorable line to translate into Chinese was a simple English one: "Explosive diarrhea of an elephant". That was almost a half-hour-long conversation between my mom and me. We were like, "We know how to say 'explode', we know the word for 'diarrhea', we sure know 'elephant', but how in the world do you put them together to create a phrase in Chinese that says, 'Explosive diarrhea of an elephant?'"

Before you go, would you like to share a funny moment with us?

I don't know if this is funny to anyone else, but there are two instances that come to mind. I knew the words for "dog" and "humping" in Chinese. But again, it was one of those times when I wasn't sure how to put it together to make it "dog-humping". So I logged another call in to mom. Now remember, she's an immigrant to this country, so she's not always hip to American slang. I actually had to explain to her what dog-humping was, "*You know, how a dog gets on top of another one and, etc., etc.*" Her reaction was "*Ohmygah, chh … Gee!*" I'm telling you, *Firefly* wound up being a great mother-daughter bonding experience. I also got to appreciate Chinese in a whole new way!

The other funny thing was meeting the guest cast and introducing myself as the person on their Chinese tapes. I met Mark Sheppard (Badger) and Christina Hendricks (Saffron) on two separate occasions. They couldn't be more friendly and gracious, but their immediate response to me was, "Oh! Pigu!" Which means butt or ass. It's not often one gets greeted with, "Oh, hi! Ass!"

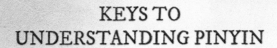

KEYS TO UNDERSTANDING PINYIN

Tonal Marks

1st tone	mā (mother)	High flat tone or even inflection
2nd tone	má (sesame)	Up tone, or rising inflection from low to high
3rd tone	mǎ (horse)	Down and up tone, or descending then rising inflection
4th tone	mà (scold)	Down tone or descending inflection from high to low
5th tone	ma (final particle used in yes-no questions)	Shortened neutral tone

Unusual Pinyin Deciphered

Letter(s)	Pronunciation is...
q	"chee" as in cheap
x	"shee" as in sheep
zi	"tze" as in ritzy
ci	"tse" as in cats
zhi	"jr" as in jury
chi	"chr" as in "church"
shi	"shr" as in "shred"
ri	"zhr" as in azure
yu	"ü" as if saying "ee", "oo", and "er" simultaneously
iu	"yo" as in Leo
o	"uo" as in "woman"

Pilot Episode: *Serenity*

Mandarin Chinese	English	Speaker
Āi ya! huài le	Oh no! something's wrong	Zoë
Bì zuǐ	Shut up	Mal
Duì bù qǐ	Sorry; excuse me?	Simon
Hún dàn	Asswipe	Jayne
Kuáng zhě de	Totally insane; acting like crazy people; nuts	Wash
Nǐ men dōu bì zuǐ	All of you shut the hell up	Mal
Nǐ tā mā de. Tiān xià suǒ yǒu de rén dōu gāi sǐ	Dammit, everyone under the sun ought to die	Mal
Qǐng jìn	Come in	Inara
Shì	Yes (affirmative)	Kaylee, Wash
Tā mā de	Damn it	Mal
Wǒ men wán le	We're in big trouble; it's all over for us; we're doomed	Zoë
Xiǎo mèi mèi	Dear little sister	Mal, Inara
Zhù yì	Watch out; be careful	Zoë

Ep 2: The Train Job

Mandarin Chinese	English	Speaker
Dǒng ma?	Understand?	Jayne
Gǒu cào de	Dog-humping	Jayne
Kě wù de lǎo bào jūn	Detestable old tyrant	Kaylee
Qǐng zài lái yī bēi wǔ-jiā-pí?	Can I have one more glass of Ng-Ka-Pei, please?	Mal
Zhè zhēn shì gè kuài lè de jìn zhǎn	This is a happy development	Mal
Zhēn de shì tiān cái	An absolute genius	Kaylee

Ep 3: Bushwhacked

Mandarin Chinese	English	Speaker
Fēng le	Crazy; loopy in the head	Jayne
Hún dàn	Asswipe	Jayne
Tiān cái	Genius	Kaylee
Tiān xiǎo de	In the name of all that's scared; heaven knows	Wash
Wǒ de mā	Mother of God; my God	Jayne
Wǒ de tiān a	Dear God in heaven; oh my God	Mal
Zāo gāo	Crap; what a mess	Wash
Zhēn dǎo méi	Just our luck; what rotten luck	Mal

Ep 4: *Shindig*

Mandarin Chinese	English	Speaker
Bǎo bèi	Darling; sweetheart	Atherton Wing
Cāi bù shì	No way	Kaylee
Gǒu shǐ	Crap; dog shit	Atherton Wing / Inara
Lǎo péng yǒu, nǐ kān qǐ lái hěn yǒu jīng shén	Old friend, you're looking wonderful	Inara
Pì gǔ	Butt	Badger
Shén me?	What?	Kaylee
Tī wǒ de pì gǔ	Kick me in the ass; kick my ass	Mal
Wā	Wow	Mal
Wěi	Hello; hey	Wright
Wén guò pì	Smelled a fart	Badger
Xiè xiè	Thank you	Kaylee
Yú bèn de	Stupid	Mal

Ep 5 : Safe

Mandarin Chinese	English	Speaker
Bù tài zhèng cháng de	Not very normal; not entirely sane	Simon
Chú fēi wǒ sǐ le	Over my dead body	Gabriel Tam
Chuī niú	Bullshit	Gabriel Tam
Dà biàn huà	World-changing	Simon
Fèi huà	Nonsense	Mal
Gǒu shǐ	Crap; dog shit	Simon
Jiàn tā de guǐ	Like hell; nonsense; preposterous	Simon
Jīng cháng méi yòng de	Consistently useless	Mal
Lǎo tiān, bù	Oh God, no	Wash
Lè sè	Garbage	Simon, Kaylee
Liú kǒu shuǐ de biǎo zi hé hóu zi de bèn ér zi	Drooling idiot son of a whore and a monkey	River
Mǎ shàng	Now; right away	Mal
Mèi mèi	Little sister	Simon
Nà méi guān xī	It's all right	Gabriel Tam
Nián qīng de	Young one	Patron
Niú fèn	Cow poop	Simon
Piān zhí de jiū chá yuán	Stubborn disciplinarian	Simon
Shuài	Handsome	Kaylee
Tiān xiǎo de	God knows what	Gabriel Tam

Ep 6: Our Mrs Reynolds

Mandarin Chinese	English	Speaker
Āiya	Damn; oh no	Wash
Bāo	Steamed, stuffed bun	Wash
Dà xiàng bào zhà shì de lā dù zi	To have the explosive diarrhea of an elephant	Mal
Dāng rán	Of course	Simon
Děng yī huí er	Hold on a second; wait a little while	Wash
Guǎn nǐ zì jǐ de shì	Mind your own business	Mal
Hún dàn	Asswipe	Mal
Jiàn huò	Cheap floozy; hussy	Zoë
Jīng cǎi	Brilliant; splendid	Wash
Nǐ bù gòu gé, nǐ hùn qiú	You don't deserve her (or you're not good enough), you fink	Kaylee
Rén cí de fó zǔ	Merciful Buddha	Inara
Wǒ de mā hé tā de fēng kuáng de wài shēng	Holy mother of God and all Her wacky nephews	Wash
Zěn me le	What's going on; what's wrong?	Simon
Zhēng qì de gǒu shǐ duī	Steaming crap pile	Bandit

Ep 7 : Jaynestown

Mandarin Chinese	English	Speaker
Gū yáng zhōng de gū yáng	Motherless goats of all motherless goats	Wash
Gè zhēn de hún dàn	A real bastard	Jayne
Hú chě	Shut up (as in "get out")	Zoë
Yē sū, tā mā de …	Jesus-mother-of-a-jumped-up …	Jayne
Xióng māo niào	Panda piss	Bartender
Zhè shì shén me làn dōng xī	What is this trash?	Wash

INARA: Mal, this isn't the ancient sea. You don't have to go down with your ship.
MAL: She ain't going down. She ain't going anywhere.

Ep 8 : *Out of Gas*

Mandarin Chinese	English	Speaker
Dǒng ma?	Understand?	Mal
Fèi wù	Junk; trash	Zoë, Mal
Gǒu shǐ	Crap; dog shit	Rival Captain
Guǐ	Ghost; hell	Jayne
Jiù shēng xì tǒng gù zhàng. Jiǎn chá yǎng qì gōng yìng	Life support failure. Check oxygen levels immediately	*Serenity* (ship's emergency beacon)
Qù nǐ de	Go to hell; screw you	Wash
Suǒ yǒu de dōu shì dāng	All that's proper	Mal

Ep 9: Ariel

Mandarin Chinese	English	Speaker
Lǎo tiān yé	Jesus	Simon
Mèi mèi	Little sister	Simon
Nǐ hǎo	Hello; how are you?	Agent McGinnis
Qīng wā cāo de liú máng	Frog-humping son of a bitch	Mal
Tiān shā de è mó	Goddamn monsters	Simon
Xī niú	Cow-sucking	Jayne
Yān guò de hún dàn	Castrated bastards	Simon

Bonus translation

Yòu tián, yòu shuǎngkuài.	Sweet and refreshing. Drink Blue	Blue Sun Corporation's
Hē Lán Rì Kělè!	Sun Cola!	jingle in ad

Mandarin Chinese	English	Speaker
Fàng zòng fēng kuáng de jié	Knot of self-indulgent lunacy	Mal
Hé chù shēng zá jiāo de zāng huò!	Filthy fornicators of livestock!	Book
Mèi mèi	Little sister	Simon
Niú shi	Cow dung	Mal
Tā mā de hún dàn	Mother-humping son of a bitch	Mal
Tài kōng suǒ yǒu de xíng qiú dōu sāi jin wǒ de pì gǔ	All the planets in space flushed into my butt	Wash
Zāo gāo!	Damn it!	Mal

Ep 11: Trash

Mandarin Chinese	English	Speaker
Bèn tiān shēng de yī duī ròu	Stupid inbred stack of meat	Saffron
Bù huǐ hèn de pō fù	Remorseless harridan	Simon
Fàng xīn	Don't worry	Zoë
Hóu zi de pì gǔ	Monkey's ass	Saffron
Kuài qù hěn yuǎn de dì fāng	Go far away very fast	Simon
Nǐ men dōu shì shǎ guā	You're all idiots	Inara
Qiáng bào hóu zi de	Monkey-raping	Mal
Shén shèng de gāo wán	Holy testicles	Mal
Suǒ xì	Petty; trivial	Inara
Tā shì suǒ yǒu dì yù de biǎo zi de mā	She's the mother of all the whores in hell	Kaylee
Wáng bā dàn de biǎo zi	Son of a mother's whore	Saffron
Yī qǐ shēn hū xī	Let's all take a deep breath	Mal
Zhàn dǒu de yī kuài ròu	Dangly piece of flesh	Zoë

INARA: Honey, you look horrific.

SAFFRON: What are you doing here?

INARA: Oh. Just my part of the job.

SAFFRON: What part of the job?

INARA: You know, I put on a big act, storm away in a huff. Then I fly off, wait for you to double-cross Mal, beat you to the rendezvous spot and grab the loot before you can get to it. What? You didn't see it coming?

Mandarin Chinese	English	Speaker
Dǒng ma?	Understand?	Lieutenant Womack
Gǒu shǐ	Crap	Lieutenant Womack
Nǐ gào sù nà niú tā yǒu shuāng měi mù?	Why don't you tell the cow about its beautiful eyes?	Kaylee
Tiān xiǎo de	Heaven knows; in the name of all that's sacred	Mal
Xiōng cán shā shǒu	Ruthless killer	Kaylee
Wǒ de mā	Mother of Jesus	Wash

Bonus translations

Jǐng tì xiǎo tōu. Zhùyì nǐ de cái wù. Zhè ge hángzhàn dào qiè héng xīn	Pickpockets alert. Mind your valuables. Pickpockets are at work in this station	Public announcement in Li Shen's Space Bazaar
Simmering Sam's jīn tiān tè jià wǔ cān, hóng shāo yútóu tang. Sì lóu, xī biān, shí jiǔ hào tān wèi	Simmering Sam's lunch special today, fried fish head soup. Level 4 West, Stall 19	Public announcement in Li Shen's Space Bazaar
Liù lóu chóng hài. Zàn shí guān bì. Suǒ yǒu shāng diàn gǎi zài shí èr lóu yíng yè. Hěn bào qiàn zào chéng gè wèi de bù biàn	Level 6 closed for vermin explosion. All businesses temporarily relocated to Level 12. We apologize for any inconvenience this may cause	Public announcement in Li Shen's Space Bazaar
Dào Devendra yuè qiú qù de dì yī jiǔ qī liù hào bān jī, zuì hòu guǎng bō. Qǐng suǒ yǒu de lǚ kè lì kè dào dì èr shí liù hào xīngjì jiāotōng zhàn dēng jī	Final boarding call for shuttle flight 1976 en route to Devendra Moon. All passengers report immediately to interstellar transport station 26	Public announcement in Li Shen's Space Bazaar
Pái zhào: líng bā èr yī hào, zōng sè huò chuán de zhǔrén, qǐng zhùyì. Nín de zhuó lù dēng hái liàng ze. Qǐng shù guān diào	Attention, the owner of a brown transport barge, register number 0821, please report to your vehicle, your landing lights are on	Public announcement in Li Shen's Space Bazaar

Ep 13: Heart of Gold

Mandarin Chinese	English	Speaker
Dǒng ma?	Understand?	Jayne
Gēn hóu zi bǐ diū shǐ	Engage in a feces-hurling contest with a monkey	Inara
Làn dàn jiàng	Weak-ass sauce	Mal
Màn màn di, rén lèi yòng jìn le dà dì de zī yuán. Huāng wú le, tā wú kě gōng yìng. Lüè duó zhě, mǎn zài ér qù. Chuàng shì jì, chǎn shēng de dà dì, shǒu dù gǎn dào gū lì. Dì qiú wèi rén lèi de róu lìn ér tòng kū liú lèi, suān kǔ de lèi shuǐ, màn liú le yī shì jì. Huǐ miè zhī huǒ, rú tiān jiàng fú zhōng yú lái dào	Little by little, the tribes used the Earth up. Barren, she had little left to offer them. Swollen of her, they left. And for the first time since the Great Burn birthed her, she was alone. The Earth cried, and terrible were her tears. Acid and caustic, the spawn of the tribes' rape, they flowed a century. The fire that finally came did so as a blessing	Play's Narrator
Mèi mèi	Little sister	Nandi
Niào shǐ de dǔ guǐ	Piss-soaked pikers	Wash
Wáng bā dàn	Dirty bastard sons of bitches	Nandi
Zhēn méi nài xīn de fó zǔ	Extraordinarily impatient Buddha	Nandi
Zhù fú nǐ, mèi mèi	Blessings on you, dear sister	Nandi

Ep 14: Objects in Space

Mandarin Chinese	English	Speaker
Bì zuǐ, ni hěn bù tǐ tiē de nán shēng	Shut up, you inconsiderate schoolboys	Inara
Fèi fèi de pi yǎn	A baboon's ass-crack	Jayne
Xiōng měng de kuáng rén	Violent lunatic	Inara

FAQ from the Writer's Desk
Monica Valentinelli

How did you get involved in this project?
I've been neck-deep in the *Firefly* 'Verse since 2012. I worked on the *Firefly* Role-Playing Game from Margaret Weis Productions, and was the lead writer and developer for several books. Between my work on the corebook and the first supplement, a Titan editor approached me for a new non-fiction project. I happily accepted and, thanks to Titan and Fox, had the opportunity to continue adding to the 'Verse.

Are there canon differences between the games, comics, and language guide?
This is, by far, one of the most common questions I've been asked ever since this book was announced. The *Firefly* canon's roots are grounded in the TV series – specifically the episodes themselves. Each additional element that's been designed to fit the 'Verse has a specific purpose like telling a story or, in my case, presenting a fabric of material so fans can tell their own stories. The intent of how canon is to be used, coupled with the realities of licensing, have resulted in some discrepancies. Thus, canon you find in this book is not intentionally designed to be compatible with other materials.

What source materials did you use?
English terms and definitions, plus notes about language usage, were based on the *Firefly* TV scripts and the writers' show notes. For the Chinese, *Firefly* translator Jenny Lynn

was an invaluable source of information, and I'm happy she was able to take time out of her busy schedule to contribute to this book.

Why didn't you include terms and definitions from the *Serenity* movie? Or the comics?
The project's parameters, due to the licensing situation, only includes the show. The movie was produced by Universal Studios, and there are slight canon differences between the show and the movie (e.g. the Blue Sun logo is different, and there are new locations and characters introduced in the film). The comics, published by Dark Horse (which is also a separate license), follow a timeline that occurs before the events of the series and after the movie. This is also why we could not reference certain details found in the movie, comics, and other resources like interviews. For example, Shepherd Book's true identity, River's safe word, and the contents of Inara's syringe are are not included in this guide.

What period do the definitions cover?
The definitions included in this language guide represent the characters, locations, objects, and events from the show. The episodes, which took place six years after the conclusion of the Unification War, roughly take place over a two-year period. The specific year and dates of the Unification War are extrapolated from the show, movie, and comics. However, the general consensus is that the show occurs between 2517 and 2518.

Why is there no ranking system for the Alliance/Independent military? Or the government?

The complete list of ranks and titles for complex organizations and schematics presented in the show were not determined by the show's writers. Military ranks and political positions are included in the terms, but there wasn't enough material to form an accurate list of rank, position, and what each entailed.

Some of the definitions based on Earth-That-Was cultures and beliefs are not a precise depiction of what they are in our world. Why is that?

The *Firefly* TV show is set 500 years into the future, and humanity is scattered across hundreds of planets and moons. The cultures and belief systems in the show are presented in context of this vast, futuristic landscape Joss Whedon and his writing team created. Thus, while there may be similarities between our world and what Whedon created for this science-fiction show, *Firefly* is a work of fiction that predicts a future inspired by our reality to make the story more believable.

Where do the crewmembers fly in the show?

Mal's focus was to keep *Serenity* in the air and avoid run-ins with the Alliance. The ship's flight path reflects this desire. He primarily stuck to the Border planets and moons to find work, but did visit the Core and rim in the show, too. Unfortunately, not every moon and planet was named in the show, and some new worlds were visited during flashbacks. During the show's main plot, the *Serenity* crew's flight path took them to: the black (*derelict ship*), Persephone, Whitefall, undisclosed

(*bar*), Niska's Skyplex (*Ezra's orbit*), Regina, the black again (*abandoned spaceship*, *Alliance cruiser*), Persephone, Jiangyin, Triumph, the black (*net*), unknown (*snowy world*, *possibly St Albans*), Higgins' Moon, Ariel, Ezra, Bellerophon, the black (*Li Shen's Space Bazaar*), St Albans and Deadwood.

Why are there discrepancies in the way some terms are spelled?

The spellings were taken from the original show scripts, and some variances were noted during analysis and editorial processes. For accuracy purposes, both versions were included.

When you wrote up the characters, why didn't you include a timeline of events and their character write-ups?

The intent for these pieces was to focus on dialogue and highlight how the characters reveal their personalities through their language. If this was a show bible or a canon reference guide, we would have taken a different approach to their presentation.

What does *Firefly* mean to you?

Firefly is one of the first properties that allowed me to marry my personal fandom with my career. I consider myself a very lucky Browncoat! To me, the show is a masterclass in how to write fantastic characters that share a common purpose but are still distinct and unique. There's conflict everywhere you look, yet this crew still manages to stay together. It's a miracle. Now that I've worked in the 'Verse, I appreciate the effort it took to tell such a wonderful story even more than I did before. Like all fans, of course, I'd love to read and see more of these characters – but now I wish I was part of those writing teams too!

CREDITS
Author: Monica Valentinelli
Editor: Nicola Edwards
Joss Whedon interview: Abbie Bernstein
Jenny Lynn interview: Monica Valentinelli
Jenny Lynn photo courtesy of: Amy Bynum
Chinese Translations: Jenny Lynn
Author Thanks: To Joss Whedon, for your
hard work and dedication to all that you do.
Thank you for being a huge inspiration! To
Beth Lewis, for giving me the opportunity
to breathe life into the 'Verse again. To my
editor, Nicola Edwards, for being amazing.
And, to Browncoats everywhere ...
Find a job. Find a crew. Keep flying!

Ballad of Serenity

Take my love, take my land
Take me where I cannot stand
I don't care, I'm still free
You can't take the sky from me.

Take me out to the black
Tell them I ain't comin' back
Burn the land and boil the sea
You can't take the sky from me.

Leave the men where they lay
They'll never see another day
Lost my soul, lost my dream
You can't take the sky from me.

I feel the black reaching out
I hear its song without a doubt
I still hear and I still see
That you can't take the sky from me.

Lost my love, lost my land
Lost the last place I could stand
There's no place I can be
Since I've found Serenity

And you can't take the sky from me.

– Written by Sonny Rhodes

爺垃圾孤羊中的孤

注意宝貝狂者的什么胡扯真倒霉

殺手廢物平靜哎呀坏了閉嘴真他媽要

統故障檢查氧氣供應你好天曉得凶

很不體貼的男生不體貼的男生救生

殘殺手是你的慢慢的闆彈醬完美貓

若木雞藍日你告訴那牛它有双美目

的狀的嫌子的媽茶快去很遠的地方她是所辜丸

進展

輕的熊貓尿太空危電氣

死能耗玩鬧手不敢加价同盟水青

鬼神聖的睪丸請進天下所有的人都

看起來很有精神懂嗎王八蛋真的是

的拉肚子凶猛的狂人是糟糕老朋友

帥老天爺垃圾孤羊中的什么胡扯真

王貝除非我死了閉嘴真他媽要命沒手廢